Mindfulness Training

Your Every Day Guide to Achieving Mindfulness and a Stress Free Life

(Increase Happiness, Decrease Anxiety and Find Peace Through Present Moment Mindfulness)

Shirley Whitney

Published by Rob Miles

© **Shirley Whitney**

All Rights Reserved

Mindfulness Training: Your Every Day Guide to Achieving Mindfulness and a Stress Free Life (Increase Happiness, Decrease Anxiety and Find Peace Through Present Moment Mindfulness)

ISBN 978-1-989990-92-6

All rights reserved. No part of this guide may be reproduced in any form without permission in writing from the publisher except in the case of brief quotations embodied in critical articles or reviews.

LEGAL & DISCLAIMER

The information contained in this book is not designed to replace or take the place of any form of medicine or professional medical advice. The information in this book has been provided for educational and entertainment purposes only.

The information contained in this book has been compiled from sources deemed reliable, and it is accurate to the best of the Author's knowledge; however, the Author cannot guarantee its accuracy and validity and cannot be held liable for any errors or omissions. Changes are periodically made to this book. You must consult your doctor or get professional medical advice before using any of the suggested remedies, techniques, or information in this book.

Upon using the information contained in this book, you agree to hold harmless the Author from and against any damages, costs, and expenses, including any legal fees potentially resulting from the application of any of the information provided by this guide. This disclaimer applies to any damages or injury caused by the use and application, whether directly or indirectly, of any advice or information presented, whether for breach of contract, tort, negligence, personal injury, criminal intent, or under any other cause of action.

You agree to accept all risks of using the information presented inside this book. You need to consult a professional medical practitioner in order to ensure you are both able and healthy enough to participate in this program.

Table of Contents

INTRODUCTION 1

CHAPTER 1: DEEP SLEEP MEDITATION 6

CHAPTER 2: REDUCE STRESS AND ACHIEVE EMOTIONAL EQUILIBRIUM 22

CHAPTER 3: FINDING YOUR "SWEET SPOT" 29

CHAPTER 4: THE INTENTION 34

CHAPTER 5: DIFFERENT TECHNIQUES 40

CHAPTER 6: BODY SCANNING 60

CHAPTER 7: MINDFULNESS AND RELATIONSHIPS 73

CHAPTER 8: MINDFUL ACTION 83

CHAPTER 9: MINDFULNESS TECHNIQUES 86

CHAPTER 10: PRACTICAL MINDFULNESS TECHNIQUES FOR REAL PEOPLE 97

CHAPTER 11: HOW MINDFULNESS HELPS YOU TO LIVE IN THE PRESENT MOMENT 106

CHAPTER 12: BREATHING MINDFULLY 112

CHAPTER 13: HOW MINDFULNESS IS HELPFUL IN DEPRESSION, ANXIETY & STRESS 115

CHAPTER 14: WHAT IS MINDFULNESS? 121

CHAPTER 15: THE TWO ARROWS 135

CHAPTER 16: WALKING MEDITATION 141

CHAPTER 17: WHAT DO YOU NEED TO MEDITATE WITH ZAZEN? 143

CHAPTER 18: ANXIETY DISORDERS 152

CHAPTER 19: RELAXATION AND MINDFULNESS 167

CHAPTER 20: DEEPER PRACTICE 173

CONCLUSION 193

Introduction

In case there is one ability that you could study that would make each and every area of your life nicer, what would it be?

Certainly, it would be the capability to manage your feelings and to manage the way you think.

This might seem like an unusual claim, but the capability to manage your feelings and the way you react to a scenario is not only the key to happiness but also the trick to being able to obtain whatever you desire from life.

Why? Due to the fact that it's our interpretation of occasions, more than the occasions themselves, that determine our joy, emotional state and performance. Not just that, but our feelings and the neurotransmitters that manage them are what changes our ability to concentrate, to recall information and to be inventive.

Let's picture a situation where you're trapped inside a lorry that has flipped over and is now looming the edge of a cliff. The tiniest movement could ruin the balance and send you falling to your death.

What occurs to you in this scenario? You freeze in place, of course, but simultaneously, your body ends up being very engaged. Your brain understands you're in danger, and therefore it causes particular neurons in mind to fire and produce neurotransmitters. These neurotransmitters include the likes of dopamine, cortisol and norepinephrine.

At the same time, the sympathetic nervous system reacts to these signs and starts creating more chemicals of its own. Specifically, a portion called the adrenal medulla will produce adrenaline and noradrenaline and this will lead to various physiological alterations in your body: your heart rate rises, your muscles contract and your brain speeds up.

But here's the twist: it appears that a rescue team has been working unbeknownst to you and has connected the lorry to the solid ground by a chain. You're entirely safe.

The response of your body is in response to your view and your perspective and not the reality.

And as we will see within this book, there are many situations where we think we're in more harm than we truly are leading to the stress reaction. And as we'll likewise see, that stress reaction is capable of triggering all sorts of mental and health issues.

If you can obtain control of your emotional reaction, then, you could stop that stressful reaction and alternatively stay cool and focused.

But the power of managing your emotions is a lot more profound than that. As we'll see eventually in this book, the capability to boost your self-confidence can actually result in all kinds of adjustments in your life that lead to you being more effective, more prosperous, even wealthier.

And it doesn't end there! Managing your emotions also implies you'll have the ability to conquer stressful situations and even fears! Bid farewell to a fear of public speaking . And also, regulating your emotions can help you to prevent arguments and shouting matches in your relationship-- which will lead to more unified and joyful home life.

Then there are the ways that your feelings can make you more dynamic and more effective. Did you know, for example, that you can boost muscle fiber employment and possibly delve into superhuman strength by entering the right mood? Did you know that the appropriate mix of neurochemistry can give you great recall?

This book is going to present you how to take advantage of all those things and simultaneously, it will show you how you can basically get some peace and quiet by soothing your brain and taking a break.

Read on and prepare yourself to change your life.

Chapter 1: Deep Sleep Meditation

As the title might suggest, this is the meditation dedicated to sleep. But what is deep sleep? Deep sleep is a profound and deep state of relaxation, where your mind synchronizes itself with Alpha frequencies, which are the most relaxing frequencies achievable by humans.

In different studies, Alpha frequencies are associated with REM sleep, where dreams are the most vivid and "realistic". Therefore, even if it is rare, I would like to tell you that some people may experience a dream-like state during the practice. Do not get frustrated if you lose contact with the awaken world, as that is the exact goal of this technique.

You can do this meditation in the evening, before going to sleep, or during the day, if you need a quick resting session between your duties.

As in every other meditation of this book, there will be some moments of stillness, to allow you to enjoy the blissful state the most. In this one, there will be particular long moments without my voice, as I do not want to disturb your sleep.

Let's get started!

Find a comfortable, relaxed and balanced position. Give yourself permission to be completely present for yourself, and let your body and mind calm down until they become soft and relaxed.

Breathe in, feel relaxed...

breathe out, feel calm...

Breathe in, feel relaxed...

breathe out, feel calm...

Breathe in, feel relaxed...

breathe out, feel calm...

Breathe in, feel relaxed...

breathe out, feel calm...

Allow the mind to distance itself from all thoughts and orientate awareness on your breath. Breathe naturally and do not force a specific rhythm. Let your breath come and go.

Carefully, now, drive your attention from the breath to the space in which you are.

Feel the energy and atmosphere of this space as it permeates all of your being. Notice the noises in the background. Maybe there is a clock ticking, maybe there are cars passing just outside your windows. Whatever you feel it is fine, let your attention rest on the external.

Breathe in, feel relaxed...

breathe out, feel calm...

Breathe in, feel relaxed...

breathe out, feel calm...

Breathe in, feel relaxed...

breathe out, feel calm...

Breathe in, feel relaxed...

breathe out, feel calm...

Now bring the attention back to the breath. Take your time and you will naturally reach a place of warmth and ease.

There is nothing to do here, nothing to think or to worry about. Just rest your attention on the breath, following each inhalation and exhalation with curiosity, falling into the rhythm of your very own body.

If you want, you can place your hands on your belly. This will help you enter in connection with the natural movement of the air entering through your nose and exciting trough the mouth.

Breathe in, feel relaxed...

breathe out, feel calm...

Breathe in, feel relaxed...

breathe out, feel calm...

Breathe in, feel relaxed...

breathe out, feel calm...

Breathe in, feel relaxed...

breathe out, feel calm...

Breathe in, feel relaxed...

breathe out, feel calm...

Breathe in, feel relaxed...

breathe out, feel calm...

Breathe in, feel relaxed...

breathe out, feel calm...

Breathe in, feel relaxed...

breathe out, feel calm...

Often times, people that struggle falling asleep just need to focus on their breath and everything will become much easier and smoother. If that is you, keep resting your attention on the air that enters through your nose. Follow its path down to the lungs and feel their expansion under your chest.

Every cell in your body is getting nourished by the air and you are getting more and more energized with each breath.

Breathe in, feel relaxed...

breathe out, feel calm...

Breathe in, feel relaxed...

breathe out, feel calm...

Breathe in, feel relaxed...

breathe out, feel calm...

Breathe in, feel relaxed...

breathe out, feel calm...

Breathe in, feel relaxed...

breathe out, feel calm...

Breathe in, feel relaxed...

breathe out, feel calm...

Breathe in, feel relaxed...

breathe out, feel calm...

Breathe in, feel relaxed...

breathe out, feel calm...

Now I will give you a few more minutes to focus on your breath. If during this time you lose connection with my voice, do not worry. This is the exact idea behind this practice. If you do not fall asleep, than no worry either, as rest has many different forms.

Breathe in, feel relaxed...

breathe out, feel calm...

Breathe in, feel relaxed...

breathe out, feel calm...

Breathe in, feel relaxed...

breathe out, feel calm...

Breathe in, feel relaxed...

breathe out, feel calm...

Breathe in, feel relaxed...

breathe out, feel calm...

Breathe in, feel relaxed...

breathe out, feel calm...

Breathe in, feel relaxed...

breathe out, feel calm...

Breathe in, feel relaxed...

breathe out, feel calm...

Breathe in, feel relaxed...

breathe out, feel calm...

Breathe in, feel relaxed...

breathe out, feel calm...

Breathe in, feel relaxed...

breathe out, feel calm...

Breathe in, feel relaxed...

breathe out, feel calm...

Breathe in, feel relaxed...

breathe out, feel calm...

Breathe in, feel relaxed...

breathe out, feel calm...

Breathe in, feel relaxed...

breathe out, feel calm...

Breathe in, feel relaxed...

breathe out, feel calm...

Letting now go the focus, allow your mind to do whatever it wants to do. There is no need to force anything, as you are now entering a deep state of pure relaxation. All the problems, the issues of daily life cannot enter this safe space. You are free to experience it in your very own way, as there is no good or bad, right or wrong.

Breathe in, feel relaxed...

breathe out, feel calm...

Breathe in, feel relaxed...

breathe out, feel calm...

Breathe in, feel relaxed...

breathe out, feel calm...

Breathe in, feel relaxed...

breathe out, feel calm...

Breathe in, feel relaxed...

breathe out, feel calm...

Breathe in, feel relaxed...

breathe out, feel calm...

Breathe in, feel relaxed...

breathe out, feel calm...

Breathe in, feel relaxed...

breathe out, feel calm...

Breathe in, feel relaxed...

breathe out, feel calm...

Breathe in, feel relaxed...

breathe out, feel calm...

Breathe in, feel relaxed...

breathe out, feel calm...

Breathe in, feel relaxed...

breathe out, feel calm...

Breathe in, feel relaxed...

breathe out, feel calm...

Breathe in, feel relaxed...

breathe out, feel calm...

Breathe in, feel relaxed...

breathe out, feel calm...

Breathe in, feel relaxed...

breathe out, feel calm...

How do you feel right now? Give yourself the space and time to welcome this question, without trying to find an answer, but just listening to your body and to what it has to tell you.

Breathe in, feel relaxed...

breathe out, feel calm...

Breathe in, feel relaxed...

breathe out, feel calm...

Breathe in, feel relaxed...

breathe out, feel calm...

Breathe in, feel relaxed...

breathe out, feel calm...

Breathe in, feel relaxed...

breathe out, feel calm...

Breathe in, feel relaxed...

breathe out, feel calm...

Breathe in, feel relaxed...

breathe out, feel calm...

Breathe in, feel relaxed...

breathe out, feel calm...

Breathe in, feel relaxed...

breathe out, feel calm...

Breathe in, feel relaxed...

breathe out, feel calm...

Breathe in, feel relaxed...

breathe out, feel calm...

Breathe in, feel relaxed...

breathe out, feel calm...

Breathe in, feel relaxed...

breathe out, feel calm...

Breathe in, feel relaxed...

breathe out, feel calm...

Breathe in, feel relaxed...

breathe out, feel calm...

Breathe in, feel relaxed...

breathe out, feel calm...

I will now give you a few more minutes to enjoy and stay in this space. Once again, there is nothing to do or to think about. Just be as you wish, knowing that good and bad, right and wrong are not to be seen during this practice.

Breathe in, feel relaxed...

breathe out, feel calm...

Breathe in, feel relaxed...

breathe out, feel calm...

Breathe in, feel relaxed...

breathe out, feel calm...

Breathe in, feel relaxed...

breathe out, feel calm...

Breathe in, feel relaxed...

breathe out, feel calm...

Breathe in, feel relaxed...

breathe out, feel calm...

Breathe in, feel relaxed...

breathe out, feel calm...

Breathe in, feel relaxed...

breathe out, feel calm...

Breathe in, feel relaxed...

breathe out, feel calm...

Breathe in, feel relaxed...

breathe out, feel calm...

Breathe in, feel relaxed...

breathe out, feel calm...

Breathe in, feel relaxed...

breathe out, feel calm...

Breathe in, feel relaxed...

breathe out, feel calm...

Breathe in, feel relaxed...

breathe out, feel calm...

Breathe in, feel relaxed...

breathe out, feel calm...

Breathe in, feel relaxed...

breathe out, feel calm...

Now bring the attention back to the body and start feeling your arms and legs once again. You can close your hands or move your fingers, just to take control of the space around you.

Please, keep the eyes closed for now and enjoy the beautiful moment you are living. You have given yourself the time to feel better and that is absolutely incredible.

Breathe in, feel relaxed...

breathe out, feel calm...

Breathe in, feel relaxed...

breathe out, feel calm...

Breathe in, feel relaxed...

breathe out, feel calm...

Breathe in, feel relaxed...

breathe out, feel calm...

Now become aware of the environment around you once again. Feel the different sounds, the temperature of the room you are in and once you are ready, open the eyes again.

Chapter 2: Reduce Stress And Achieve Emotional Equilibrium

What exactly is emotional equilibrium? Exact answers may vary as everyone is unique, but if you are able to manage almost any situation in a positive, optimal way, you have achieved emotional equilibrium. Mindfulness techniques can help you reduce levels of stress and feel balanced and equipped to handle all areas of your life, whether physical, emotional, or a combination.

How exactly is mindfulness effective in attaining emotional equilibrium?

Stress is one of the enemies of emotional equilibrium. Using mindfulness techniques will enable you to understand and reduce stress in your life, develop a healthy, achievable routine, become more familiar with your body, and also understand your weak points, struggles, as well as your strengths. Mindfulness techniques will shed light on your emotions.

As you understand your emotions and stress triggers, you can use mindfulness techniques to analyze them in a noncritical way. When you achieve emotional equilibrium, you do not attempt to bury your emotions. You will analyze your feelings and use mindfulness techniques to decide the healthiest, most positive way to process your emotions.

Why is it important to strive for emotional equilibrium, and what changes will I notice in myself as I achieve it?

As you master mindfulness techniques, you will increasingly be able to focus your thoughts and emotions on the positive. Emotional equilibrium is a state of mind which empowers you. You will feel good about yourself, your choices, your possibilities, and you will manage events and situations with less stress and more confidence.

When you learn the mindfulness techniques which allow you to reach emotional equilibrium, you will find your stress levels are reduced, and you can handle your anger better. In addition, you can practice forgiveness, which releases negative energy from your body and allows your mind to focus on positive emotions. You will find forgiving others is a gift to yourself, and the ability to truly forgive is much easier when you have emotional equilibrium.

Which mindfulness technique is most recommended to realize emotional equilibrium?

There is a mindfulness technique that, once mastered, is particularly effective in achieving emotional equilibrium. It will be described in the following section. Emotional equilibrium is an incredibly valuable skill to master, but it takes training and practice. As you learn more about emotional equilibrium, you will understand the importance of working through your feelings one at a time, and being able to concentrate on one objective before working through the next.

Achieving mindfulness techniques specifically focused on your emotions can give you a renewed, positive outlook, enabling you to approach emotional challenges with a fresh, optimistic attitude. As you develop a routine, you will incorporate mindfulness practice into your life much like a daily exercise regimen.

What are the steps used in the mindfulness technique for emotional equilibrium?

The steps are not difficult. You should be in an area free of distractions. Make yourself comfortable. Feel yourself relax, releasing any tension in your shoulders. Close your eyes. It is time to concentrate internally. Begin with your basic breathing exercises, counting your breaths from one to ten. You are going to focus on each breath, breathing in through your nose, filling your lungs, then exhaling out again.

Take your time, and when you feel ready, think about the particular emotion that you have been experiencing. Your emotion can be either positive or negative. Recall what event triggered that emotion.

As your eyes remain closed, continue to think about that emotion, remembering the events and feelings you had. Relive the situation in your mind, recognizing the existence of every thought and feeling that flows through you. Recognize that you may be feeling more than one emotion.

Examine the event from all angles, trying to determine what caused the situation. You do not want to deny any emotion. Feel your physical response to the event as you recall it. Recognize any sensations, such as a rapid heartbeat or sweating. Acknowledge that the way you are feeling is normal. You should not feel stress, nor should you feel guilt. You want to fully accept the emotion or emotions, recognize and identify them, and then return to focusing on your breathing. When you are ready, open your eyes.

How long will it take to notice results and improvements from mindfulness on my emotional well-being?

You will detect certain results almost immediately. Just increasing your awareness of your body is a step toward emotional equilibrium. True emotional serenity and equilibrium will occur over time. It is necessary to practice mindfulness a minimum of once per day, and to focus on ridding yourself of negative emotions. Negative emotions undermine the state of emotional equilibrium. Worry, fear, stress, anger, and depression are associated with the presence of negative emotions. It takes time to work through your emotions, but with practice, you will achieve emotional equilibrium.

How often and at what time of day should I practice this mindfulness technique?

What time of day to practice mindfulness to achieve emotional equilibrium is up to you. It is important to practice at some point every day, and sometimes it is advisable to practice more than once per day. The goal is to acknowledge and accept your emotions, and in doing so, stabilize your emotional state. It takes practice and consistency to achieve this balanced state of mind. Achieving emotional equilibrium using mindfulness techniques is a long-term goal, and will require continued effort and awareness on your part.

Chapter 3: Finding Your "Sweet Spot"

Everything in life is about balance and harmony. Whether you are creating an amazing food recipe, making music, juggling with life's responsibilities and commitments, your ultimate goal is always to find your "sweet spot" and to trial and error a "center point" in the midst of everything. Picking the right notes, right proportions of ingredients, and then mixing it up to achieve a certain texture, a certain taste, or a specific melody that fits the lyrics to the song that will strum the strings of your heart. Anything out of balance feels out of whack, feels unpleasant and overwhelming. It just doesn't sit right when you're not in your "sweet spot".

Meditating is the same thing. In the beginning, it would be extremely awkward, even to the extent of having certain levels of discomfort in the physical body caused by the attempt to give the mind new instructions to take it slow, to let it all go. Any kind of environment we were growing up with, be it work or school, or even at home, you were conditioned to take in as much as you possibly can, to grow up quickly and learn as fast as you possibly can. To absorb, and to digest.

No one in this world ever taught you to let go. To do less, and to not do anything at all. To just be present and be in the moment. You would never find it in any "to-do list" because it seems "lazy" to have so little on it. To fathom the concept of doing less, yet able to be producing more. In this day and time, quality productivity surpasses any other forms of multi-tasking. You can be the best multitasker in the world but at the end of the day, if you went home and unloaded your "overflowing" cup and drowned everyone else with your workload you have taken on, then you have not succeeded in finding the balance and harmony for yourself.

You are simply dumping it off on someone else. A best friend, a lover or a spouse, your poor mother, or perhaps even strangers who have no business listening to you ranting on about your day's issues. This is why we practice mindfulness to find the "sweet spot". It can increase positive emotions and lower negativity, and thus counteract stress and prevent depression from "overworking" the mind. It also increases the capacity for attention (to be present) and develops our memory, so we may put our focus on the good things in life that we already have. Of course, being mindful helps to be more solution oriented and getting better at exploring creative strategies for problem-solving. Meditation also helps a person withstand the traumatic effects of the mental state of being and enhance its resiliency.

Mindful living benefits us in a positive way which we are able to experience our bodies and minds differently and we are not so quick in reacting to bad situations and circumstances, instead, we will be able to handle it effectively and positively strengthening ties and relationships with every aspect of our lives. It can extend to every aspect of our existence and consistent practice will lead us to benefit from it in the long-term immensely. The "sweet spot" equates to "life's satisfaction".

Mindfulness cultivates behaviors and attitudes that encourage it and makes the pleasures of life more noticeable and enjoyable, also helps us become more committed to activities in the moment and a greater capacity to deal with life's challenges and curve balls thrown in our way. All of these ultimately leads to greater overall life's satisfaction. So we get more done and feel really good about it, which ultimately reduces the moments of "default thinking", allowing the mind to wander off carelessly.

Being present in the moment lets us learn to become more flexible in our thinking, less stubborn and resistant to new concepts and ideas. We can observe our thoughts without becoming overly attached to them against our own will, we're able to accept them without the attempt to change them or have it be different. There is a deep sense of well-being that is sturdy and stable, not having to be dependent upon life's circumstances which are ever-changing at an unpredictable rate. We will be able to thrive in the harshest of conditions with a practiced mind, sitting in our "sweet spot".

Chapter 4: The Intention

In the previous chapter, you learned about the importance of intention when you are being mindful. Intention and purpose define the difference between mindfulness and simply being in a state of awareness. Initially, mindfulness is hard. You will not be able to achieve it all at once, and it may take many months or even years to become mindful in all areas of your life. As you practice these new patterns and intentions, however, you will find that it becomes more instinctual for you to become mindful in your everyday life.

The above quote emphasizes that we are all here with a limited amount of time to be around. We only get so many journeys around the sun before we expire. Knowing that, there is no sense in making one moment more special than the next. Instead, we should do our best to be purposefully mindful of all moments and find peace and happiness in them as much as we possibly can. Like the fish in the drying well, we are destined to die, and therefore why would we waste our time putting any single moment on a pedestal over the rest? Whether the moments you hold dear are ones that have passed or ones that are yet to come, it is best to acknowledge them for what they truly are: moments that no longer exist. There is no purpose in letting yourself use these moments as a means to suffer. Instead, acknowledge them and then bring yourself back to the present moment as much as you possibly can. Eventually, it will become easy to do so.

When you are seeking to live in a mindful state, you should realize that you aren't actually seeking to live in a constant state of happiness. That in itself would draw away from your happy experiences and dilute their value in your life. Instead, mindfulness is the practice of living a more peaceful existence. When you live this way, you will result in having heightened levels of success in multiple areas of your business because you are able to think objectively and thus make objective decisions in your life. This mindset allows you to eliminate the actions we take as a result of emotional baggage as allows you to think more clearly and make decisions that will have a more positive result on your success in life overall. This success will be experienced not in just one area of your life, but in all.

When you are mindful, you may feel as though you are living in a state of delayed gratification. In this day and age, we are all about instant gratification and often find ourselves reacting to everything from an emotional state of mind. As a result, many of our actions are emotionally charged and are not done with our highest benefit in mind. This is the case when we are not living in a state of mindfulness. Oftentimes people turn to selfawareness as a "quick fix" instead of putting in the necessary work to become mindfulness as a whole. We think that simply noticing something within' ourselves is enough, and giving adequate attention to that part of ourselves is not necessary.

It is not enough, however, to simply become self-aware. Doing this may allow you to know yourself more, but it will not allow you to take total control over your mind and shape it in the way that you desire. Mindfulness allows you to purposefully act with intention and objectively make decisions. Instead of being self-aware that you tend to get angry when a certain thing happens and then recognizing your angry response, you will recognize that anger and then start to understand the trigger. You will then learn to heal that trigger within' yourself and as a result you will be able to look at the trigger objectively in the future. Instead of reacting with an emotionally charged reaction, you will respond with an objectively considered response.

Mindfulness means that you will be operating in a way that will likely remove the instant gratification from most things that you do in your life. However, it will encourage a long-term sustainable state of peace that will bring you more in the long run. Instead of chasing fleeting moments of gratification and experiencing periods of suffering in between, you will teach yourself to live in a permanent state of peace that will eventually become void of those intermittent periods of suffering. As a result, your life overall will be more fulfilling with peace and in many cases, happiness.

As you read about mindfulness, especially based on the Buddhist and Dharma teachings, you may feel as though you need to go to the extent of becoming a monk and dedicating your entire life to mindfulness teachings. This is simply not true. You can live in a mindful state no matter who you are, no matter what religion you follow, and no matter where you are in life. There are no boundaries on who can practice mindfulness in this way.

Chapter Summary:

- No moment is more valuable than the rest, all are valuable to your growth
- Acknowledge each moment for what it truly is
- Setting intention allows you to consciously direct your mind
- Mindfulness eliminates instant gratification but introduces long-term gratification
- You do not need to be a monk to benefit from or achieve mindfulness

Chapter 5: Different Techniques

As people may know, meditation has countless benefits, and everybody seems to be giving it a try. A look at any book on meditation either online or in a bookstore will show you that there are many ways of meditating, different types of techniques and also a lot of conflicting information on the subject. People will naturally speculate what method might be best to practice meditation. Not all meditation techniques are the same or even similar. Some of the meditation techniques will work for you while others won't. This means it is a manner of trial and error you have to get the method that works best for you. With thousands of techniques to try, you will, for sure get one that works best for you. There is no singular approach to meditation, which is why it is vital that you test the various methods and see what works for you. It is possible that the person that teaches you meditation will give you many options, and it is your body and mind to choose the best.

Focused Attention Meditation:

In this method, you focus on a single object for the whole session. You might be focused on your breathing, a visual object, part of your body, or any other external object. This way, you don't get distracted easily, and you will keep the flow when the attention to the object gets stronger, and your mind gets clearer. The best thing about this method is that you won't have to go through many distractions. Due to this, you will develop better depth as the attention gets steadier. Some of the common examples of focused meditation practices include Buddhist meditation, chakra, sound, kundalini, and many others.

Open Meditation:

Here, you don't have to focus on a single item so that you can make your mind clear. Instead of putting all you to focus on a single object externally, the practitioner keeps his mind open for the possibility of finding the best item that you can focus on and get to your goals. To get the best object, you need to consider all the aspects of the experience, and while you are at it, you avoid making any judgments or attaching to any object. You have to see any emotion that comes your way the way it is without attaching any meaning to it.

Zen Meditation:

Zen (Zazen)

In Japanese, Zazen translates to "seated Zen" or "seated meditation." Zen originates from Chinese Zen Buddhism, and it goes way back to the 7th century. This type of meditation technique can be done by both new as well as seasoned meditators. The biggest benefit of meditation is that it gives you an insight into the working of the mind. This type of meditation will benefit you in a variety of ways that include giving you the necessary tools to cope with anxiety and depression. However, the deepest benefit of using this type of meditation is to give you a deeper spiritual connection, because you will get to uncover the workability and innate working of your mind. This will be an experience like no other.

Let us look at the various benefits that you can enjoy:

Tackle Deep-rooted Issues

When you opt for Zen meditation, you will be able to tackle deep-rooted problems and get answers to general life questions that you have never found answers to. The answers you get will be based on logic and study.

Get permanent Solutions

When you go for Zen meditation, you don't get temporary answers to questions; rather, you will be able to address the many core issues that take you down. The practice will point to the main cause of issues and will make sure you get the best solutions to issues. If you have been in a mindful class, then you understand that the secret to happiness lies way deep within you. You will be able to be aware of yourself and then connect better to other people.

Achieve Calmness

On a better level, you will train the mind to be calm. As a mediator, you will be able to reflect on your life with better focus and be more creative. Due to this, your health becomes better, because your blood pressure might go lower and your immunity might improve. With better calmness, you can sleep better and reduce stress levels.

Breath Observation

When running a meditation session, you need to assume a comfortable posture. Get a comfortable mat or a cushion. When you are comfortable, you can then focus your attention towards an object of the meditation. Then go ahead and observe your breath, specifically the way you inhale and exhale. This will foster a sense of alertness and presence.

Quiet Awareness

Here, you allow your thoughts to flow through your mind without rejection, judgment, and grasping anything. It is also called "just sitting," and the meditation is done without an object to focus on.

When you meditate, you don't have a goal. All you do is to sit and allow your mind to wander.

Intensive Meditation

This is ideal for group meditation, and it is ideal for temples and meditation centers. During the meditation, you will devote most of your time to sitting down and trying to connect with your deeper mind.

Every session lasts anything between 30 and 50 minutes, and you will alternate the session with meals, breaks, and walking meditation. Al meals or any other activity is handled in silence. This type of Zen is more common in Japan, Taiwan, and the West.

Awareness Meditation:

This form of meditation is seen as the way to know yourself. The aim is to give you an insight into the real nature of your experiences. The meditation style has been around for 2500 years, and it started when Buddha found out that insight, knowledge, and goodness form the basic answer to suffering and dissatisfaction. This form of meditation seeks to get you to connect to the inner you when you look inside yourself, you get to know that fulfillment and joy is a nature that you cannot run away from.

This form of meditation is the right path to gaining insight. This means that anyone can practice this technique and make the best out of it. Even if you are of a different faith, you still have the capacity to make things work for you.

The Technique

You get to practice the technique in two methods mindfulness, which is also called Samantha meditation, and vipassana, which is more of awareness.

Samantha Meditation

This is focused on gaining the peaceful dwelling, mindfulness, and tranquility that you can use to focus on an object. Usually, the main object to focus on is your breath. When you meditate, try to identify the thoughts and emotions that will come in when you are in the thick of things. However, don't dwell on the emotions, let them go. Once you get the hang of not having to attach on some objects and emotions, you will relax.

Vipassana Meditation

This one builds on the various aspects of Samantha meditation. It is usually seen as insight or awareness meditation. Once you have learned to move past your emotions and thoughts, you can now move to look at the qualities that come with a better perception of things, consciousness, and more. When compared to Samantha, you will be more active in your thoughts. To get the best out of the meditation technique, you need to get guidance from an expert that will analyze you before making a decision.

Specific Sensations

Once you have developed the right sensation using Samantha meditation, you will develop the right form of calmness by practicing mindfulness and presence. You will get to focus your mind on a specific aspect of your normal experience. Let us look at the different aspects that you can focus on.

Sitting —when you decide to sit, you will start to focus your attention to the actual sensations that come with breathing exhaling and inhaling.

Walking —when you go for walking meditation, you will keep your attention on touch and movement sensations of the feet and legs.

Eating —you can use eating to make your meditation work for you. The primary object in this instance is the taste sensation. Many times, we eat when we are talking with other people or checking our messages, but when we eat when we are silent, we end up doing it with little or no distraction.

Mindfulness Meditation:

When you decide to be mindful of the surroundings, you will be able to achieve more than you can ever achieve when you aren't aware. Whether you are handling stresses from work and personal life, you will be able to deal with them much better if you become aware of your environment. When you are mindful, you will be able to steady your mind, have clear thoughts, and manage a lot of stress that will come your way. Let us look at the various breathing meditation techniques that help you to slow down things better, help you make better decisions, and then boost your productivity.

One-minute Relaxation breathing

This form of meditation is ideal when you feel pressured, anxious, or panicked. It is also ideal when you need stress relief and immediate intervention for your issues.

When you regulate your breath, you get the capacity to lower your blood pressure fast and effectively. Relaxation breathing is all about exhaling longer than you inhale. This means the body signals itself to rest and digest so that you can relax from the inside out. You will be able to control your responses to various stresses rather than reacting in an impulsive manner.

<u>The Process</u>: When seated in a comfortable position, take a deep breath then count to four as you hold your breath, and then exhale for double the time. While you inhale, make sure you feel the oxygen go into the system. Repeat this several times.

7-minute Breathing Meditation

This meditation gives you better focus, improves attention, and gives you a better sense of clarity and calm with time. Being mindful is all about trying to disengage yourself from the thoughts and images of the past and then avoid the resulting stress and rumination. When you go for mindful breathing meditation, you are using your breath as the center of the session. You have to concentrate on the sensation and the rhythm of the breathing. You are all about forcing your awareness in such a way that you stay focused.

The Process: Make sure that you sit in a comfortable position with your spine nice and long. Begin counting your exhales by counting up to ten, then counting back to one. Do this for five cycles, and you will realize you are breathing in a calm manner. When you do this, make sure you visualize the breath moving through your system and appreciate the way it moves through your system.

Body Scan – 5-minute Meditation

You can use this form of meditation to be aware of your body and ease the tension that develops after a long day at work. You can also use the process to fall asleep at night. This kind of meditation allows you to identify where the patterns that keep you from relaxing exist, and then you release them with your awareness. This makes sure you relax better.

The Process: Sit in a comfortable position and then take the time to get a steady breath. Next, bring the awareness to the various sensations to the body, and use slow breaths to find your bearing. As you move the air within your body, try and look for areas that have a lot of tension and then push your breath into the area. Make sure you push the breath into the different sides of the body.

Mantra Meditation:

Mantras refer to objects that are used in meditation. They are very common and powerful, as well. This type of meditation is found across the world. It is used in both wisdom traditions as well as secular meditations as well. Mantra is a word that comes from two Sanskrit phrases man, which means to think and train, which means to be free from. When putting together, the phrases mean the tools of the mind.

Most of the mantras get their power from the sound quality that they possess. Many of the mantras are composed of single syllables, while others are composed of many words. Mantra meditation works through recital and listening to the mantras. You can say them fast or say them slowly, at times you repeat them, or at times you say them just once. You can even connect the mantras to certain feelings, your breathing, abstract concepts, or visualizations.

So, what role does the mantra play when you meditate?

First, the mantra comes in as an object that you focus on. It acts as an object that will make your mind busier and get it to be centered and calm. This means it will work the same way you focus on your breath in another form of meditation. Secondly, the mantra works as a tool for transforming your consciousness. Each mantra comes with a certain quality that will aid you produce consciousness and different states of the mind when you repeat it for a long time.

The Benefits of Mantra Meditation

This form of meditation comes with various benefits for the practitioner. You might be skeptical about repeating words, but let us look at the various reasons why it is seen as a powerful tool in meditation.

Sound Produces Vibrations

If you have been in any alternative treatment program, you know that vibrations are always used to help relieve tension and many other things. The sound comes from vibrations. The cells that produce sound vibrate in a certain rhythm to give you the sound that you produce. The thought and feelings in your body are just vibrations that go through your consciousness and your body.

When sound passes through the fluids in your body, they affect the secretion of hormones, behaviors, cognition, and psychological well-being. Vibrations can help change all your emotional states such as uplifting your moods, soothing of pain, and overcoming your anxiety. It can also help to access the deeper states of your consciousness and control the mind. Sound also goes a long way on evoking thoughts, moods, and emotions. So, using mantra makes it possible for you to rotate your consciousness around a particular sound, making sure you amplify it for maximum effect at all time. In many forums, this form of meditation is seen to be the easiest and most effective of all of them.

It Replaces Thinking

Mantra can take thinking to a whole new level. Usually, the common type of thinking is when you are distracted by many thoughts and other objects, but when it comes to mantra meditation, you desire to focus only on one thing the whole time. The method is pretty simple you pay full attention to the mantra, and you aren't disturbed by any other memories, thoughts, and sensations. Another good thing is that the nature of the mantra overrides those songs that usually play in your mind continuously during the meditation process. This usually doesn't happen in other meditation forms.

The Process: Choosing the Right Mantra

You have to choose which kind of mantra to work with – this can be spiritual or secular. The one that you choose usually affects the results that you get from the process. The good thing is that come mantras are universal and you can use them with both processes.

Secular Mantras

When you go for secular meditation using the mantras, the approach is seen as a tool that you use to grow, enjoy better health and performance as well as to relax. You can use the mantras even when you don't believe in anything that is spiritual. Alternatively, you might believe in the spiritual world, but you don't want to mix religion with meditation.

This way, you get to choose a mantra from your language or any other thing that isn't religious. When choosing a word, follow the guideline below:

Look at the meaning. Choose a phrase or a sentence that represents what you wish to develop more within yourself. Let it help you to connect more to your inner self. Some examples of words to use include peace, freedom, courage, etc.

Avoid negative words and phrases.

Don't just jump on any mantra that comes your way; rather decide on the one that usually speaks to you. Once you get one that is the best, you can keep on using it so that it becomes more effective.

Taoist Meditation:

This is a practice that originated in China. The method was used in ancient times to heal the body and the mind. Taoism is a meditation method that is followed by millions of people across the world. Many followers have made it become recognized as a religion, though many people regard it as a philosophy. Taoism focuses mainly on concentration, mindfulness, contemplation as well as visualization. Although many other forms of meditations are akin to Tao meditations, they aren't alike. In Taoism, you get to move physically, and you meditate spiritually. The meditation focuses so much on the energy, which makes it different from Buddhist meditation. The process has a close correlation to the Chinese martial arts as well as Chinese medicine.

Qigong Meditation:

This meditation method uses both physical and active meditative elements to help you balance to strengthen and preserve your inner power. The meditation exercise will help improve your immunity, relieve you from stress, and alleviate specific physical and mental conditions. This meditation method bases its effect on the ancient practice of the same, and for many beginners, it can be confusing and intimidating. The practice will involve capturing the energy in your body by utilizing energy pathways that are called meridians to allow energy to flow through freely. If there is a blockage in the system, then you will experience an ailment that will occur in the areas of the body.

Chapter 6: Body Scanning

Mindfulness meditation begins traditionally with a mental body scan where you sit on a chair so you sit well and do not fall apart. Sit with your right back so you carry yourself, ie Without leaning back against the backrest. Put aside. A pillow between the waist and backrest so you support there. Lift the breastbone and make your shoulders slide back relaxed. Make your neck long and bend your back slightly down to the chest. The body now forms an S-shape from the tailbone into the loin, beyond the upper part of the back, the neck - and over the head where the garden bends slightly down to the chest.

Sit with your feet firmly in the floor straight ahead and with a little distance in between. The hands rest on their thighs.

Come mindful present right now and now

Close your eyes and feel for a moment your entire body, from head to bottom. Feel your breath - is it deep or is it short short breath? ... Is it regular or irregular?

Now turn your full attention into the room around you. Register the entire room, from wall to wall. How is the air in your room - cool or hot against your skin, moist or dry? ... How is the smell in the room? ... Register all sounds around you. ... Have full attention to where you are right now and here. Without judging it as good or bad. Now you're right here right now.

Now turn your full attention into the body again. Recognize your breathing. Now focus on the outer space in the nose where you breathe the air in and out. Feel how the air you breathe is a little cooler than the air you breathe, it's a little warmer.

A body scan lasts approx. 10 minutes. Body scanning gives you a better feel of your body. And it coaches you consciously moving your focus from place to place in your body. If you feel difficult to feel the body, exercise is even more important. And you'll get a little better each time.

The cleansing breath

The cleansing breath stimulates your wellbeing both mentally and physically and gives new energy.

Pull the breath deep and slowly through the nose. As much as you can. Now breathe slowly through the mouth. As much as you can. Until you are emptied of air all the way down the stomach. Only then do you pull back the air through the nose and exhale through your mouth. Take at least 3 deep cleansing breaths.

Focus your mind - count your breath

"Thrush breathing" is a meditation form where you concentrate your entire awareness of counting your breath. When you concentrate on the breath and count it, use this as anchor (focus point) for your consciousness. The anchor helps you not to let you go away and away in your mind -

into past or future. - Wake away right now and here.

Practice

Spirit in and out through the nose. Feel the air filling your chest and your stomach - and notice how the air leaves your stomach and chest and expands through the nose. ... Begin counting your breath on every breath, like this: Spirit in, spirit out: 1. Spirit in, spirit out: 2, etc. Count up to ten and start over at 1 - over and over again.

If you lose the count because you are distracted by thoughts, start from 1 onwards and continue to count up to 10. Again and again.

Stay alert and fully focused on your breath and the countdown.

Mindfulness meditation

Attention to Attention - Meet yourself with calm observation and acceptance.

The so-called consciousness-expanding meditation is the true mindfulness meditation where you become aware of your attention.

Before doing mindfulness meditation, prepare yourself and your mind through the previous concentration exercises. Otherwise, you will have too many thoughts and it will not be rewarding to you.

Where ever you concentrate fully on breathing and counting to exclude everything else - all your thoughts, feelings and impulses - do not exclude anything in this exercise. On the other hand, you are aware of what is happening in your consciousness. You observe closest to yourself "from the outside". You observe all the thoughts and feelings flowing through your consciousness. You become more aware of yourself - about what's going on in you. Thought patterns that repeat. You experience how many random and often indifferent thoughts are filling you. Thoughts and pictures that bring you back in the past or out in wish and dream about the future. Everything that awakes old feelings and may longing for you. Everything something that removes you from being right now and here.

However, in mindfulness you do not judge or judge yourself. You do not judge the thoughts or feelings that may arise. But you just observe everything. You accept every thought, every picture or feeling that comes up in you. And then you let go and return to your anchor, that's your breath.

Mindfulness meditation: you do that

Side with closed eyes. Turn your attention to your breath. Feel the air flowing in and out through the nose.

Observe now ... If there is a thought or feeling through you, just register. Accept it - whether it's uncomfortable. Then let go of it by returning to full breathing attention.

When you're pulled away by a new thought or feeling, do the same again. Register it, accept it. And let go of it by returning to the breath.

Sit for a few minutes now.

Stay alert and alert. Always remember: your breath is your anchor.

Slowly, you are now out of this meditation.

Round with 5 cleansing breaths. 5 deep breaths through the nose and 5 even deeper exhale through the mouth.

Come back slowly to common consciousness. Gently massage your hands and your face. When done, open your eyes.

Mindfulness mediation in the form of the term "relaxation" is very effective if you decide to have sleep problems, for example as a result of stress. A longer and more detailed version of body scanning can be recommended if you want to sleep well.

Meditation as you go - with full attention

Normally when we go for a walk we let the mind go. Some become creative and poetic. Maybe we enjoy nature or we are in a conversation with a friend almost without changing the surroundings. It is common sense of everyday life, in which we follow long and often random thoughts, which may end all directions.

When you are fully aware, you are fully aware of your attention. You do not let it go away now and here. Out in creative ideas. Back in your past or in the future. However, when you suddenly find yourself in thoughts and images about the past and the future - and it will happen many times - gently turn your attention back to now and here by feeling your breath. When you consider your surroundings, you are aware that this is what you are doing right now.

On one of your walks you can do the following: Take some comfortable shoes and go for a walk - like a place without so much traffic - in nature, in a park. Just a place where you can concentrate. Feel the air against your skin. The heat or coolness. Register scents. You are now turning your full attention to your breath. As you walk, you notice how you through the nose pull the air into your lungs and stomach and how you breathe - even through your nose. Feel the movements of the chest and the stomach with the breath. Let the weather draw itself: you do not affect your breath, but lets it flow in and out of you as it is.

When driven away from the moment of thoughts and images, register it, accept it and gently turn your attention back on the breath.

Now you turn your full attention into your feet. Feel the feet against the ground you walk on. How to put the heel in the ground and start again with the front part of the foot and toes. Feel the movements of the feet. Do not know mentally to see a picture of your feet, but by noticing them. Already now you will automatically slow down.

Keep on feeling your feet. It will soon give you a quiet grounding. Try to feel both your breath and your feet at the same time. Is it difficult, it can help go into a rhythm where you count your breath and create a rhythm with your steps. For example, breathe in 3-4 steps and spirit out to 4-5 steps. So a little longer exhalation than inhalation: Spirit into 1,2,3,4 spirit out 1,2,3,4,5.

In this way, your mind is fully focused and you are master of it.

Take this full attention for a few minutes at a time. You can now choose when you want to go full alert and when you want to go with regular everyday awareness. The important thing is that you consciously choose when you do the one thing and the other. And so do it.

You train yourself to control your mind and become master of it. In choosing which state of mind you want to be in. From moment to moment.

Mindfulness also coaches your reactions: impulse control

Are you a day, for example, frustrated, restless, restless, depressed, sad, want to smoke, drink alcohol, or want to conflict with a particular person, mindfulness training helps you to better manage your Mind and your thoughts. Mindfulness meditation gives you peace of mind, reduces stress, and controls your thoughts, feelings and reactions. You will be able to accommodate your feelings by registering them, accepting them and then gently leaving the feeling by turning your full attention to your breath. In this way you can accommodate your feelings and thoughts so that you do not have to be "slave" of them.

If you have the urge to respond to an instant impulse, you have a way to get back to yourself, move your consciousness away from what you need, thus mitigating the need. You can thus postpone the act of turning on the smoke or buying the drugs. It gives your room and option to choose a completely different solution that is better for you in the long term - and that does not give you any hassles and problems the following day.

Are you following the exercises to get back to your breath, etc. Still, urgency and urgent need for support, you may call someone near you, a friend, one in the family. All focus shifting is impulse control. Ie You expose inappropriate actions so that you have the opportunity to choose something that is better for you in the long term. You can also take a shower, go for a walk, take a place where you care. Do something that works well for you.

Completion of meditation

It is important always to come quietly out of mindfulness meditation. So keep your eyes closed a bit yet. Move your attention to the whole body as you also did to begin with. Massage your hands a little and your face. Move your toes and feet slightly. And now come slowly for ordinary everyday consciousness, when you're ready, open your eyes. Notice if you feel clearer and calmer in your consciousness than before.

Pay attention to attention

Where concentration is narrow, focused and excludes everything except the subject of your concentration, the attention in mindfulness is open, unlimited and can accommodate all the impressions. For example, if you focus all your attention on breath, the mind is concentrated on breathing - but if you are aware of both your breath and catching the shift in your attention when your concentration is drowning - then you're what's called mindfulness in mindfulness.

In mindfulness, we withdraw the attention as if we are standing behind ourselves and observing all that is happening in us. We consider it all and contain it all uncritically.

Attempt to perceive every thought, every sense, every recording of sounds, visual impressions, touches, body sensations, etc.

Chapter 7: Mindfulness And Relationships

Majority of us suffers from a disease of always thinking about ME rather than thinking about the US. We just think about our existence. We rarely find time to think about our existence as a part of a society.

Most of our thoughts include "I" rather than "WE." When we have some free time, we mostly think like this: "I want," "I like," "I wish" and "I think" etc. The problem with the Western culture has been the same. People in the West, for centuries, have been considering themselves as individual identities and it leads them to focus on "I" factor. In comparison, people in Asia and Africa considered themselves as the part of a bigger whole, community, so they are accustomed to focus on "US" and "WE" factor.

West had given the individual so much importance, first in Italy and then during the renaissance movement in Britain that people's focus shifted to the individuality. The social system in the West grew on the same lines. Individual freedom extended so much that people had to focus on their own prosperity. Machiavellian school of thought also contributed to this concept.

In Africa and Asia, people depended on the community because they did not have enough resources and tools to depend on their abilities largely. Lack of latest knowledge also raised concerns about social security and that is why they developed a sense of unity to feel stronger and safer.

Our thoughts are so much influenced by the outer world that we don't focus on the common aspect of the human society. This is why our relationships feature selfishness, ignorance, greed, and jealousy. There are different ways in which we spoil, the relationships.

Why do we like our success but hate other's success? Just because our thoughts trick us by telling the mind that anybody else, with success, will gain more authority and importance and grab more attention. Why do we love seeing others lacking behind and why don't we like ourselves lacking the behind? We actually like to see the world's reality by sitting at a distance. We love to see how suffering works, but we don't want to be the victim of it.

Most of us love horror movies, but how many of us love to be in a real-life horror situation? Our mind feels the sensation of miseries and joys. But, when it comes to the miseries. We just love to practically experience joys, but we hate being a victim of miseries even though our mind loves this sensation when it happens to somebody else. This is why we love survival movies, gladiator-fight recreation and circus jugglers risking their lives. Simple, we like what is good or our existence, and we hate what is bad for our individual existence.

Relationship Mindfulness

For relationship mindfulness, we first need to be a sensitive enough. For this, we need to follow a simple routine, every day:

- I am like everybody other in the world
- Everybody other in the world is like me
- If I feel pain, everybody another feels pain
- If I feel sorrow, everybody another feels sorrow
- I like to eat well so does everybody
- I have the right to prosper, so does everybody

Sit in the chair and close your eyes. Start to feel your breath for a couple of minutes. Now, visualize a lousy situation, maybe an accident, bad news, the death of a person, etc. Now visualize the person who is suffering from that situation. Visualize yourself standing at a distance and watching the sufferer. Slowly focus on the sufferer and think as if you are approaching him or her slowly. Don't let your mind distract and focus on the misery of that situation and in the meanwhile associate yourself with the sufferer. Slowly, envision the suffering individual staring at you as if he or she wants to say something. This is the time when you need to imagine the feelings of that individual. This exercise could be tough but will become easy with frequent practice. Once you imagine the feelings of the victim of an adverse event, try to maintain your focus on his or her feelings for at least 10 to 15 minutes.

This imaginative journey will let your mind associate your individual being with the people around you. This is the technique which triggers the sense of sympathy, and you'll start thinking well about others around you. It triggers the sense of welfare, and this is the positive sign because it will eradicate jealousy. It will enable you to enjoy the joys of others and share their grief. When you feel the grief of others, it means that you'll no more find pleasure in other's miseries. This is what God expects from good human beings.

I just shared the simple routine to feel the miseries of others, and you must be wondering about sharing the joys of others. But there is no effective technique to practice it through such meditation. To share the joys of others, you need to develop a habit of sharing GIVING. You can do this by giving a toffee to a child on the street. You can help someone needy. Your attitude needs to be such that you become a helping hand for others. This is what makes you a skilled person who wants to see others happy.

This world is for everyone not just for you. Someone's success doesn't mean your failure. I have seen some people who become jealous of the success of their friends. This habit plays havoc because jealousy only harms the jealous. We need to be mindful of the fact that the success of our friend or relative basically promotes our family or friendship circle. We need to be generous enough to welcome the progress and feel it our own. It is only possible when you are ready to sacrifice "ME" attitude and adopt "WE" attitude.

Romance

Romance is one of the most complex relationships because of the twists in behavioral patterns. One needs to be mindful of the causes. A man needs to be aware of the biological and sexual issues of the women. A woman needs to be aware of the biological causes behind certain behavioral aspects of men.

In romantic encounters, lovemaking or physical interaction becomes complex. People are afraid of some many things. Premature ejaculation is one of the most significant issues. Women are often found complained about the inability to discharge because of their men not being able to satisfy them for long enough. These issues are primarily due to biological and hormonal causes, but there are some psychological implications as well. Viagra or other such medications are not the permanent or healthy solution. The best thing is to know the psychology of lovemaking.

The best approach is to be mindful of every touch. Sex is like eating something. If you eat in a hurry, you are not going to enjoy the taste. Same is the case with sex if you do everything mindlessly and in a hurry, nothing is going to work as planned. You need to engage in the conversation, and both partners need to know what is ahead, but still, they must not reveal. Just enjoy the conversation and teasing in the beginning. It is just like rising temperature gradually on the low flame. Spend sufficient time in conversation and then shift to the touch stage. Do not run through the body in a flash. Feel and let other partners feel each breath, sigh, and touch, kiss and smooch. People who directly jump to intercourse, do not find success because there is no psychological involvement which could make them feel the pleasure. Romance is not about animalistic intercourse, but it is about feeling the whole process and stretching it as long as you can.

Parenting:

Parenting is perhaps the most amazing, emotional and beautiful experience, as far as the relationships are concerned. You need to be highly mindful being a parent. Children are highly sensitive, and they note every response, and it stays in their minds as well. People are so busy in their routine lives that they sometimes ignore the emotional requirements of their kids. They work hard to provide better food, luxury, comfort, and shelter but in the meanwhile, they fail to comply with the emotional requirements. We need to be mindful of the kid's desire to be loved, played with and listened to.

The best technique to be a mindful father or mother is to enter the childhood world. When you are with your kids, there is no reason for having a severe outlook. You need to laugh with the kids, jump with them and behave just like a kid. It looks funny or exotic, but it works. It is like the mature human being to become a kid in the company of the kids. But we have changed ourselves so much during the centuries that scores of people around us have forgotten this instinct.

Kids do like the emotional attachment. If you fail to comply with the emotional requirements, your kids would love their pets, puppies, teddy bears and toys more than you. You might not realize this factor by the time it started, but a stage will come when you realize how great your mistake was and how easily you could have avoided it.

In the next chapter, we are going to learn the importance of mindful self-transformation by eliminating the bad habits and understanding the shift in relationships.

Chapter 8: Mindful Action

It is common for our mind to create shortcuts when we are doing seemingly unimportant tasks. When we take a bath for instance, we no longer think about each action that we need to take. Instead, our mind wanders off as our body operates in autopilot.

We try to prevent our mind from wandering off when we try to reach the state of mindfulness. When we are in this state, our mind should be on at the present moment. We should not be entertaining thoughts about the past or about the future. Instead, we should keep our mind in the task that we are doing.

You can practice mindfulness when doing menial tasks by following these steps:

Choose an activity in your routine that you do every day. For instance, you can choose one of your hygiene tasks like taking a bath or shaving. You could also choose tasks related to home maintenance like doing the dishes or organizing your stuff.

Put the activity as a regular part of your schedule. If you choose to use this technique when bathing for instance, you should find a time slot in your schedule when you will take your baths. You should ensure that you put your activity in a time slot where you will not be in a hurry.

When you are about to do the task, you should stand up straight and take 3 deep breaths. After that, you should start doing the task. When doing so, you should think of each action that you do. We usually do not do this because we let our body run under autopilot.

As you do each action, you should keep your senses focused on the task that you are doing. When washing the dishes for instance, you should focus your eyes on the plates or utensils that you are washing. When taking a bath, all your senses should be focused on the body part that you are washing. When we are doing menial tasks, we are often tempted to multitask. Many people for instance have the habit of watching the television or talking on the phone while washing the dishes.

You should keep practicing this exercise until your chosen task is completely done.

By doing this activity, you will train your mind to become more focused on your tasks. You will improve your focus and at the same time, you will remove thoughts that may cause you constant stress.

As you begin to practice this technique in multiple areas of your life, you should also try to make it a point to avoid multitasking. When we multitask, the quality or effectiveness of our work is usually affected. At the same time, when we multitask, our progress in our task becomes slower.

These effects create unnecessary stress in our minds. By following the exercise above, you will actively avoid multitasking. You will prefer doing one task at a time. As a result, you will improve your quality of work.

Chapter 9: Mindfulness Techniques

In our busy cut and thrust lives, our minds are being constantly pulled in different directions, leaving our emotions and our thoughts scattered all over the place and leaving us stressed out, anxious and, in some cases, highly strung. Most of us can't even find 5 minutes to stop, sit down and forget about everything, let alone the time we would need for a session of mindfulness meditation. However, finding time for your well-being is vital. The few minutes it can take you each day to clear your mind and learn how to see your thoughts can help you to achieve a positive balance between your body and mind and it can help you to see everything clearly.

These are some simple mindfulness techniques, designed to fit in with a busy life; designed to help you empty out your mind and find a calm spot in the storm of your daily life:

Mindful Breathing

You can do this while standing or sitting, however, you are comfortable, and you can do it just about anywhere and at any time. All you need to do is be quiet and still and focus on your breathing for just one minute. Here's how to do it:

Begin by breathing slowly in and out. Each cycle should be about 6 seconds. Breathe in deeply through your nose and then breathe out slowly through your mouth. Allow your breath to flow in your body and out again effortlessly.

Release your thoughts for just 60 seconds. Forget about everything you have to do later in the day, or anything that needs your attention. Just let go and be still for just one minute

Concentrate on your breath. Focus all your senses on your breath as it goes into your body and invigorates you, then watch it as it exits your body out of your mouth and dissolves into the world around you.

Did you think that you would never be able to learn how to meditate? If you can do the above, then you are halfway there. If you can master this for just one minute, move on and try two minutes, or even three.

Mindful Observation

This is a very simple yet very powerful exercise, designed to connect you with the environment around you, to notice its beauty. We tend to miss what is going on around us when we rush around and this will bring everything sharply back into focus for you. Here's how to do it:

Pick on one natural object that is in your immediate environment. Focus on it; watch it for a couple of minutes. It may be an insect, a flower, the moon, and the clouds, anything that is in your natural environment

Do nothing else but focus on this object, notice everything about it. Relax for as long as your levels of concentration allow. See the object as if it were the first time you have ever seen it, ever truly noticed it. Explore the object visually; look at every aspect of it and how it is formed and allow yourself to be completely consumed by the object, to the exclusion of everything else. Connect with the energy that flows from the object and connect with the purpose and the role of the object in the world.

Mindful Awareness

This simple exercise is designed to teach you how to be aware of simple tasks that you do daily and to be aware of the results that are achieved by doing them. Most of us go about our day without truly noticing what we do and this will teach you to actually be consciously aware of everything.

Think of something that you do every day, several times a day. Perhaps something that we take for granted, like opening the door. When you touch the door handle, stop. Be aware of where you are, of your feelings at that exact moment. Be aware of where the door is going to take you. If you choose turning on your computer as your object of focus, the minute you have started it up, stop and think about your hands enabling the process and your brain that helps you to understand how to use the computer.

You don't have to do this with something that is physical, like a computer or a door. Let's say that you are one of those people that have many negative thoughts throughout the course of the day. Whenever you have one, stop. Give that negative thought a label – call it "unhelpful" and then release all that negativity.

When you walk past the bakery in the morning and smell fresh bread, stop for a minute, think about how lucky you are to be able to enjoy good food and share it with your friends and your family.

When you choose your touch point, be it physical or mental, choose one that is important to you on that day. Don't go through your daily life on autopilot. Stop every now and again, think about what you are doing and where you are going and become aware of everything.

Mindful Listening

As well as not noticing what is going on around us visually, we tend to also block out sounds because we are too busy to hear them. This exercise has been designed to help you open your ears, to listen to what is going around you without judging it. Much of what we hear and see every day is influenced by things that have happened in the past so we need to learn to listen mindfully, to hear sounds without any preconception about them, to hear them as though it is the first time.

Pick a piece of music that you have never heard before, perhaps something that is in your own music collection or something that is truly new to you.

Plug in your headphones and close your eyes. Forget about judging the genre of the music, the artist or the title before the music begins to play. Instead, forget about labels and allow yourself to truly listen to the music, to follow its journey for the entire duration. Explore the track fully, even if it isn't something that you would normally listen to. Forget about any dislike that you may have and become fully aware of the track and the sound waves.

The idea here is to listen, to become entwined with the music without any judgments or preconceptions.

Mindful Immersion

With this exercise, you are going to learn to be content in the moment, to forget about the constant striving that you do on a daily basis. Instead of needing to get routine jobs done anxiously, you will learn to see that regular task and experience like you have never done before.

For example, let's say you are cleaning house. Instead of mindlessly rushing through it, desperate to get to the end, concentrate on it and pay close attention to every single detail of every single chore. Instead of seeing it as a mundane chore, see it as something completely new by taking note of every single aspect of what you are doing. When you sweep the floor, feel the motion, become the motion. When you wash the dishes, feel the muscles that you are using. When you clean the windows, take note of everything you do and find a better way to do it. The idea is to build up your creativity and find new experiences inside the old mundane ones.

Instead of pushing through each task tiredly and wishing to get to the end of it make yourself aware of everything you are doing, of every step you are taking and immerse yourself completely in it. Take that activity and make it something more than mundane or routine; physically and mentally align yourself with it; spiritually align yourself with that job and you might just find that you actually enjoy it.

Mindful Appreciation

In this final exercise, I want you to take notice of just 5 things out of your day that you normally do not appreciate. These can be people or they can be objects, it is entirely up to you. Write them down and, at the end of the day, check them off as appreciated and noticed.

The idea is to be able to appreciate and give thanks for things that seem to be insignificant but actually aren't. These are the very things that support us, our existence but we rarely give them a second glance, let alone a thought, as we rush through our busy lives, striving for bigger and better.

Take electricity, for example. The only time you really think about it is when you have a power cut and you haven't got it. We never stop and think about the fact that, without it, we could achieve so little in our daily lives. Something as simple as a cup of coffee in the morning would not be possible.

Think about the postman who gets up at the crack of dawn to deliver your mail; thin about the clothes you wear that keep you warm, that make you look good; thin about your ears that let you hear the wonderful birdsong and your nose that lets you smell that coffee and the roses.

Ask yourself these questions:

How do these things come to exist?

How do they work?

Have you ever really stopped and said thank you for the fact that you benefit from these things?

Have you ever stopped and wondered what life would be like without them?

When was the last time, if ever, that you really noticed the small details about them?

Once you have picked your five things, make it your job, no, your duty, to discover everything about them and to appreciate how they allow you to go about your daily life.

Chapter 10: Practical Mindfulness Techniques For Real People

You've now got the nuts and bolts of why you really should incorporate Mindfulness into your daily life. The time involved to do a Mindfulness session is nil compared to the benefits.

Now it's time to learn some practical Mindfulness techniques.

We've already gone over a very simple Mindfulness exercise in the beginning of this book, and being mindful can actually be even simpler than that.

You can be mindful in a very informal way. Any **thing** that you do, and devote your full attention to, is being mindful. So, things like walking, doing the dishes, doing the laundry, standing, focusing on a hobby… anything you do where you focus on only the task at hand, is being mindful.

Then there are the formal methods to being mindful. This is when you set aside time to purposefully be **mindful**.

First, a note on posture. There are some professionals that swear by sitting with an erect spine. Others say you can sit comfortably or even lay down. Do what feels good to you. If you **don't**do what feels good to you, your focus will be taken from being mindful and preoccupations of how your posture is will be more prevalent. That takes away from being mindful. ☐

Franne will usually sit in a comfortable chair or in a bed propped up with a pillow under her knees; and Dana says that she practices Mindfulness everywhere! "Seated or lying down. Walking or practicing yoga. If seated, comfort is key. I usually sit on the couch, or against the headboard of my bed, shoulders above my hips, back and legs supported. If doing a guided meditation, I lie down and place a pillow under my knees"

The most basic way to "do" Mindfulness meditation is simply to lay or sit, pay attention to your breath, and when you start to think of something other than your breath, simply go back to focusing on your breath. Don't judge or beat yourself up for thoughts entering your mind. That's natural. It's going to happen. Just let them go and focus on your breath.

You can also choose to repeat a mantra instead of focusing on your breath. A mantra is a word of words that mean something to you. By repeating the word, you focus on that word.

Some common mantras are:

Om – pronounce like "home" without the "h" (resonates most closely to your spirit)

Peace

Love

Now

As I Am

Follow

Right Here Right Now

Etc.

Yet another Mindfulness technique is what is called a body scan. You start with either the top or the bottom of your body and notice each place – your toes, feet, shins, claves, knees, thighs, all the way until you get to your scalp.

There are also some active ways to be mindful, and those are exercises like yoga and tai-chi. Here is what Dana said about yoga and Mindfulness, when asked why she started to practice Mindfulness:

"It [mindfulness] wasn't something I consciously chose. I feel like it chose me. I don't remember why I went to my first yoga class, I just knew that I had to go. Something about it felt good to me. And sometime in those first two years of practicing yoga I learned the powerful effects of mindfulness. I noticed how active my mind was, how judgmental my thoughts could be, and how choosing to bring my awareness back to my breath, back to the pose, calmed me. It also empowered me. I realized I was not my mind, or my thoughts, and that just because I had a thought, it did not mean that the thought was true. I realized I had choices. I could choose what I wanted to think about, and what I wanted to believe. And most importantly, I could choose where to place my awareness. That simple shift in my awareness changed my life."

All of the above are Mindfulness practices you can do right now. No further action required on your part. You can also search on YouTube and find a plethora of guided Mindfulness meditations, and those are wonderful as well.

Now, let's talk about fitting small moments of Mindfulness into your day. These are all very simple to do and easy to fit into your day – no matter how busy you are.

* Before you get up from your chair, stop and take a few deliberate breaths and focus on your breath.

* Before starting any new activity, take a few breaths to put an official end to the prior activity, and a focused start on the new activity.

* Set an alarm on your phone and when it goes off, do something Mindful.

* When you receive a text, or hear an email noise, use that as a "Mindfulness Bell", and take a moment to be Mindful before checking your technology.

* Mute (or pause) the TV during commercials and be Mindful then.

* While in the shower, focus on how the water feels on your skin, the temperature, the moisture, and imagine that shower washing all of your negativity, stress, anxiety, and worry down the drain.

* Being mindful is simple. Take a few deep breaths, focus on your breath (or mantra or body sensations) and when your mind wanders, gently allow yourself to refocus on your breath (or mantra or body sensations).

This is all so simple, right? You may be wondering how you are really supposed to **feel** while being Mindful. Again, let's turn to our experts. They answered the question, "How does mindfulness make you feel while you're doing it?"

"When I do it I feel centered and embodied rather than scattered and distracted." Franne D.

"Calm. And in that calmness I feel peaceful and powerful. At peace with myself, and in my mind and body, and empowered by my ability to choose to direct my awareness and energy where I want it. Being more mindful allows me to observe my thinking from a neutral point of view, and it assists me in being present to, and more accepting, of what is." Dana C.

I will attest to what they are talking about. There is such pleasure in finding a place that is not filled with stress and anxiety. And then, after a while, it becomes a place to go to reflect on you, as a person. You will find how important that is as well.

Time Commitment

"Commitment is what transforms a promise into reality." ~Abraham Lincoln

When you are feeling stressed or anxious, or worried, taking time out to practice Mindfulness can seem like the last thing you want to do. The good news is that you don't have to take an hour a day, at 3pm sharp, to reap the benefits. Mindfulness can happen any time. Any place.

"At the moment, I do not have a set schedule. To me, mindfulness is an on-going practice that I engage in throughout the day to consciously create a space that allows me to be more present to what is happening within me and around me. Sometimes my practice is proactive and preparatory, and other times it is process-oriented and healing. And sometimes I like to just be. The prompt may be an activity I am about to engage in, such as sitting down to write, or preparing myself for a healing session with a client. And sometimes I am prompted, or triggered, by thoughts or feelings that don't feel good to me. Taking time to practice mindfulness in that moment, or as soon as possible, allows me to return to that place of greater peace inside of me." Dana C.

Dana continues about how long a session normally is for her. "It can be anywhere from a few minutes to an hour or more. It really depends on the situation. The longer sessions are healing related or involve being in a yoga class or out in nature. When I choose to sit, for no other reason than to just sit, 20 minutes feels good to me."

Franne adds, "I am shy to admit that I do not have a set time, although I am ready to commit to one. Recently I have used my energy level as a signal to meditate or be still. Usually it happens mid-afternoon. It can be 10-20 minutes or as short as two or three or even a moment or two. I aim for 15-20 minutes."

Chapter 11: How Mindfulness Helps You To Live In The Present Moment

When you first take up mindfulness you are asked to sit in a position that is good for your spine. The reason for this is that your energy points or chakras are aligned and this helps you to gain more energy. When you have blocked chakras, these can cause all kinds of problems in your life. Being in the present moment, you will be asked to breathe in a certain way. Your concentration is on the breath and therefore you don't have time to think about past transgressions or things that have upset you. You are asked to put aside a simple 20 minutes a day to meditate or practice mindfulness consciously and the effect that this has on the rest of your life is astounding. It becomes a way of life, rather than something you can pick up and drop at whim.

When you are posed in a seated position with your feet flat on the floor, this helps to ground you to this moment in time. In yoga they have several exercises that help to ground you in a similar way. You may be asked to place your hands in a certain pose. The pose I use is to place my right hand on my lap – palm facing upward and then to place the other hand inside it, palm facing upward and then touch my two thumbs together.

With mindfulness practice, at first it's better to work with your eyes closed so that you don't get too much distraction. You breathe in through the nose and while you are breathing in, feel the air filling your gut rather than just the top of the lungs, as you count to 8. Then you hold onto the breath for a moment and then exhale to the count of 10. You can try lower numbers if you find this difficult and work your way up to higher numbers but the ratio stays the same and you always breathe out longer than you breathe in.

What's happening when you do this is that you are in the moment because your thoughts are focused upon your breathing. Imagine the breath like flames so that you can actually feel them coming into your body. When you breathe out, feel the air leave you. Your sympathetic nervous system kicks in and you will feel this in other areas of your life later on because this is the system that controls your body heat as well as making sure that the air you breathe gets to all of the right places. Your 20 minutes a day will help you to take your mind of being anywhere else other than the moment that you are in. The problems happen when your mind is allowed to wander off. If this happens during your meditation session, you simply observe the thoughts and then let them go. The one thing that you never do is place any judgment on the thoughts or let the emotional part of your thinking process kick in to let those thoughts have any effect on you at all. They are simply thoughts. They cannot hurt you unless you allow them to. Mindfulness stops them from having any impact on your life. You live in the moment because it's a better place to be and will find yourself doing this at random times during the day to bring yourself out of the general funk of life. There is so much invasion these days, both from social media, television and outside influence that the mind is never allowed that space it needs to be able to be present in the moment.

For example, when you are walking through a park, often you do so without even noticing anything because your thoughts are thudding away at your head in an uncontrollable way. What mindfulness allows you to do is to step away from that anger or that anxiety and to simplify what you are seeing in that moment in time. For example, you see the trees, the plants, and the birds. You see the sky and you use all of your senses to gather information about the very moment that you are in. You become more observant and when you live in the moment, you also find that life is a lot more fun.

When you are in the moment while you eat, you actually start to feel all the tastes and textures of your food and are tempted to buy fresh foods so that you can not only get the goodness but you can enjoy the moment of eating.

You listen more because your ears can pick up so many inspirational sounds. Your sense becomes much more honed and it's not only the senses on the surface. Your sense of intuition is also honed when you quieten down your mind and simply balance yourself in this moment in time. It's such an enjoyable feeling that it can help you to overcome anger and all the negative feelings that human beings experience. The key thing that helps you to stay in the moment is knowing that this moment may be the last one you ever get. If you make the most of it in positive mindfulness, you will be able to enter the next moment with the right mindset to feel happy and contented. Stop dragging your past around with you and let go because when you learn to live in the moment, life offers you so much opportunity that you may never have otherwise found.

Chapter 12: Breathing Mindfully

The purpose of mindfully breathing is to simply be aware and accept your breathing. It's not about relaxing the body or stress reduction, but this can often be a byproduct of breathing mindfully. Breathing is something that everyone does, if you have a pulse, then you are someone who breathes. Your body will know how to do this because it's been doing it since you were born. Breathing is something we do and carry with us everywhere, but we're not usually aware of it.

1. Find a chair and sit quietly in it with both your feet on the ground and your hands placed on your lap. Let yourself feel centered on the chair. Bring all your attention to just the act of breathing. Begin to notice the breath while it enters your body through your nose and make its way to your lungs. Notice with some wonder whether the inner and outer

breaths are cold or warm, and become aware where the breath goes as it enters your lungs and departs your body.

2. Be aware of the breath as your lungs exhale and how it feels when you inhale through your nostrils. Don't try to control your breathing in any way, just notice it and pay attention to it as you're aware of it. It doesn't matter if your breathing becomes slow or fast, shallow or deep. It is what it is. Allow the body to do what it does best naturally.

3. You'll begin to notice that every time you inhale, the diaphragm or the stomach expands, and every time you breathe out the stomach or diaphragm will relax. Don't attempt to do anything, just be aware of the physical sensations of inhaling and exhaling. If you find your thoughts are intruding, then that's alright. Don't worry, just notice them and allow them to exist, and then gently bring your awareness back to the breath.

4. Begin this exercise for just five minutes and build up daily over a longer period of time. You can do this exercise if you're lying down in bed if you suffer from insomnia. It's just a way that you can be more mindful and conscious of the awareness that's in your body and the surroundings. It's breathing and the capacity to relax. When your breathing relaxes, the muscles relax, too.

Chapter 13: How Mindfulness Is Helpful In Depression, Anxiety & Stress

What exactly is Depression?

Everyone feels sad or blue occasionally, usually lasting only a little while and pass within a few days.

Approximately 7% of adults in the United States may encounter major depressive disorder every year. During lifetime, women's are 72 % more likely than men to experience depression. Experts say depression is caused by a combination of factors, such as the person's genes, their personal experience, psychological factors and biochemical environment.

Suffering from depression is a serious condition/illness that makes your life feel dull and thus, your enjoyment of daily existence becomes impossible.

Depression plays traps on you. It tells you that things are sad, making you forget that there is happiness. It tells you life is pointless, when there is satisfaction and adoration to be found. It tells you that you can't do anything, when you can make a move regardless of your sentiments. It tells you that there's no chance to get out, when there is a way out. Our common reaction to feeling discouraged is to attempt to figure out how to feel better. This sounds sensible yet it sets us off on an unending circle of concentrating on our emotions and attempting to alter them specifically with our psyche. By and large, this doesn't work. By being mindful of the present moment, solutions to the problems you are facing will appear.

Our emotions vary - all sentiments, including discouragement. We perceive this methodology. We acknowledge whatever emotions emerge. We quit battling with the sentiments we don't care for and bring them with us as we go about our work on the planet. As we figure out how to coincide with our discouragement, the despondency loses its control over us.

We overcome sadness through acknowledgement, action and reason.

*You have lost your voracity or you can't quit eating

*You can't rest or you rest excessively

*You are substantially more bad tempered, irritable, or forceful than normal

*You can't focus or find that beforehand simple undertakings are presently troublesome

*You're expending more liquor than ordinary or participating in different neglectful conduct

*You feel sad and defenseless

*You can't control your negative contemplations, regardless of the amount you attempt

If you relate to, or have in the past, any of the symptoms mentioned above, you have likely suffered from depression. Numerous individuals with a depressive sickness never look for treatment.

Don't be sad! Try learning relaxation and stress management. Try stress reducing methods such as meditation: progressive muscle relaxation, yoga or tai chi to overcome from depression. Most importantly, do your best to be mindful of the present moment.

What exactly is Anxiety?

Anxiety can be defined as an emotion which is characterized by a displeasing state of mind. It always comes with nervous behavior, like pacing forth and back, rotating a pen, physical symptoms such as rapid heartbeat or excessive sweating etc. Anxiety can be defined as expecting a future threat.

Anxiety is generally overreacting to a normal situation where you feel that something you are not prepared for will occur. Sometimes it is appropriate, however if you are frequently anxious, you may suffer from anxiety disorder. An excellent way to deal with anxiety is to return to the present moment, and being mindful. An easy way to return to the present moment, is to take deep breaths (into your belly, not the chest) through your nose, and to hold your focus on that pattern.

How is Anxiety different from fear?

Anxiety and fear are both quite different. Fear can be described as being afraid of an idea or an individual. For example, a person may be fearful of being alone, swimming in the ocean, falling in love or of spiders. This is constant in the person's mind. However, anxiety is to be afraid of the unknown. For instance, a person may experience anxiety before giving a speech, talking to a person who they deem attractive, or taking a test. This is because the person who experiencing this state of anxiety is uncomfortable with not knowing the outcome, or the future. Due to this, anxiety becomes a defensive mechanism for a person, which urges them to avoid or escape from whatever it is they are scared of. When a person is completely present, and in the moment, all fear and anxiety in the mind will dissolve. This is because you cannot be completely present in the moment while focusing on the past or the future. While in the present moment, you can only focus on what is going on now!

Anxiety and fear are both unsatisfactory things for a person to live with. The true solution for dealing with these feelings, is to learn how to be mindful. By learning how to be mindful, a person gains an incredible sense of power. They can begin to take control in their life again, and experience life's incredible potential. Mindfulness meditation is the best technique to stay in the present, but it takes plenty of practice and patience to actually feel the benefits.

Chapter 14: What Is Mindfulness?

What is mindfulness? It is not a common word in most people's daily vocabulary but it is a word that is gaining popularity in recent years.

According to the Oxford dictionary, mindfulness is defined as "a mental state achieved by focusing one's awareness on the present moment, while calmly acknowledging and accepting one's feelings, thoughts, and bodily sensations, sometimes used as a therapeutic technique."

That is a huge definition. In simple English, mindfulness is simply being in the present moment and experiencing life from one present moment to the next; being aware of your own stream of consciousness. Mindfulness is really just taking time to slow down and "be in the moment". Smell the roses, dance in the rain, feel the raindrops hit your cheeks. Appreciate everything in life - feeling and experiencing everything.

"Mindfulness is paying attention in a particular way: on purpose, in the present moment, non-judgmentally," according to Marsha Lucas, Ph.D, psychologist and author of Rewire Your Brain for Love.

In today's fast-paced society, many of us lead lives that are moving at 100 miles an hour. Work deadlines, bills, mortgages, health issues and many other issues weigh a ton on our shoulders. Mindfulness helps us to make sense out of all the stresses and pressures of our lives. It helps us to focus on the important things and give thanks for the many blessings that we sometimes take for granted. Mindfulness is taking time to review our lives regularly so that we don't forget what we have to be thankful for. It helps us to focus on the really important stuff instead of some mindless "noise".

Though mindfulness is firmly rooted in Buddhism, it is in its simplest form, about moment to moment awareness of being **in the present moment**. It is not about thinking, it is about **being** – being aware. Most of us live in our heads and we are either living in the future or in the past. "What am I going to do and what will be the results of my work? What did I do and what did it accomplish?" These are the questions we are constantly asking ourselves.

Mindfulness is choosing to focus on the present and my awareness of the present. "What is happening in my environment right now – in my mind, what am I aware of right now – around me and within me?" These are the type of questions you will be asking if you are being mindful. When we meet new people for the first time we almost always ask – "What do you do?" Can you imagine what the response would be if you asked "Who are you right now?" or if we answered the question "How are you?" mindfully and honestly?

The essence of mindfulness is simply awareness and consciousness. Focusing your attention on yourself and the people or things in your presence in a specific moment in time. It is about being in relationship with your own experience with others, and with yourself. We will be looking at some exercises that you can do on a daily basis for you to get into this habit of conscious mindfulness.

The practice of mindfulness might sound easier than it really is. Remember that mindfulness is being in the moment without judging. For most of us, it is very hard to let go of judgment. Mindfulness means we notice our thoughts and feelings but we make no judgment about them or about anything else. We have to let go of the belief that there is a right way or a wrong way to feel or to think about something.

There are many things that we can do to ease into the habit of mindfulness. A simple thing that you can do is to stay focus in the present moment no matter what you are doing. Regardless of whether you are taking a shower or a walk around the block, playing with your kids or eating your dinner, you can practice being totally present in the moment without passing any judgment on anything. Simply enjoy the flow of water against your skin, the smell of your shower foam, the sensations that you feel as you rub your back or enjoy the taste of the food in your mouth, the feel of the hot soup or the crispness of your salad with juicy bits of pomegranate bursting in your mouth.

Mindfulness is a practice that has been around for ages. In Asia, it has its roots in Buddhism but in North America and Europe it was Jon Kabat-Zinn who popularized this concept and created the mindfulness-based stress reduction (MBSR) programs for therapists, schools and businesses. Today, mindfulness or meditation is often used in complementary therapies for stress management, personal development as well as various forms of health and alternative therapies. The practice of mindful meditation is used in psychiatry and clinical psychology to help reduce anxiety and depression, stress, drug and alcohol addiction. It is used by many psychologists and health practitioners as a means to help clients regain balance and inner peace in their hectic lives today.

Life-Changing Insights from Oprah, Giselle, Will Smith & Other Business Leaders

Who can practice mindfulness?

Who should practice mindfulness?

Do I need mindfulness in my life?

Do you constantly feel anxious?

Are you suffering from any physical ailments?

Are you constantly on the go?

Are you in an unhappy relationship?

Do you have compulsive behavioral issues? Binge eating? Addiction?

The truth is, mindfulness will benefit everyone, the old, the young, the healthy, the diseased, the high-flying corporate executive, the full-time mom at home looking after kids, the talented artist or even the small business owner.

Mindfulness is a fantastic way to improve our quality of life. Daily mindfulness keeps the practitioner aware of their feelings, thoughts and the environment. It also promotes self-love and encourages our acceptance of our current state without any judgement. Instead of worrying over an endless to-do list or beating ourselves up over a mistake in our past, mindfulness keeps one focus on fully experiencing every moment of every day.

Mindfulness is a way of being, a lifestyle, and a new way of experiencing life.

There have been major innovations in the use of mindfulness including in education, business, and medicine. In the medical arena there are so many advantages for mental health, stress and anxiety reduction in our lives. Losing our attachments to thoughts and outcomes as well as things can have a major impact on reducing cardiac diseases, inflammations and even stress related cancers. Studies are showing that there are actual changes in the structures of the brain that are positive and might even delay or prevent mild brain impairments or the onset of Alzheimer's disease. Conditions such as obesity and chronic pain are also positively impacted by the practice of mindfulness.

Some of the most influential people in the world practice mindfulness.

Deepak Chopra, MD, Jerry Seinfeld, Bill Ford, Larry Brilliant, Oprah Winfrey, Paul McCartney, Will Smith, Dalio, Padmasree Warrior, Tiger Woods, Clint Eastwood, Robert Stiller and Arianna Huffington. All of them practice some form of meditation.

These are all leaders in their respective fields of business, entertainment, sports, art or literature. More and more successful people from different arenas are starting to practice meditation because they are enjoying significant benefits in their lives and work. We also see more and more Fortune 500 and

Fortune 100 companies incorporating and encouraging employees to participate in activities such as meditation, yoga or self-discovery retreats.

The results these businesses are experiencing include more creative employees, higher productivity, increase in insightful engagement from employees and less absenteeism. Companies getting involved include AOL, Aetna, Google, Ford Motor Company, Apple and many more.

Padmasree Warrior, the Chief Technology Officer of Cisco Systems meditates daily and stays off all digital electronics every Saturday. Warrior says that meditation was a key for her in her previous job where she was managing over 22,000 people. Meditation was her "down" time and kept her grounded. Warrior shared that she was calmer after practicing meditation.

Tony Schwartz from The Energy Project has been meditating for many years. He started doing meditation so as to calm his mind and achieve mental stillness. Schwartz has written several books, blogs and articles on mindfulness. He finds that mindfulness helps him and it helps his employees to improve their work performance.

Many people do not know that Oprah Winfrey practices meditation. Oprah practices stillness for 20 minutes each time at least twice daily. She believes so much in the power of meditation that she has brought in teachers for any employee wanting to learn the art of meditation. After a meditation retreat in Iowa last year, Oprah said, "I walked away feeling fuller than when I'd come in. Full of hope, a sense of contentment, and deep joy. Knowing for sure that even in the daily craziness that bombards us from every direction, there is -- still -- the constancy of stillness. Only from that space can you create your best work and your best life."

A couple of other examples from the world of business include the CEO and founder of Salesforce, Marc Benioff, who is a great supporter of meditation and mindfulness. He offers this insight, "I enjoy meditation, which I've been doing for over a decade -- probably to help relieve the stress I was going through when I was working at Oracle". The CEO of Linked In, Jeff Weiner, is another fan of this ancient art. Weiner fills his twitter feed with positive comments on meditation and mindfulness. Weiner is passionate about everything that has anything to do with meditation and mindfulness.

Arianna Huffington, the 52nd most powerful women in the world (Forbes 2014) and the founder of the Huffington Post, is an avid yoga and meditation practitioner. She offers weekly classes for employees of both the Huffington Post and AOL (Huffington Post was acquired by AOL in 2011). She is a major advocate of mindfulness and often speaks of its health benefits as well as its impact on bottom line. "Stress-reduction and mindfulness don't just make us happier and healthier, they're a proven competitive advantage for any business that wants one," she wrote in a recent blog.

Giselle Bundchen, super model and wife of New England Patriot quarterback, Tom Brady, has been practicing meditation for years. Like Oprah, she also meditates twice a day for about 20 minutes each time. Giselle uses meditation to empower her to stay positive in different stressful situations. Following the birth of her first child she used it to regain her pre-pregnancy weight and shape. Giselle has shared that mindfulness practices helped her to lose her baby weight in a mere two months. She has also been known to enter into three days of mindful silence without talking to anyone.

Like so many others in Hollywood, Ellen DeGeneres also practices meditation. DeGeneres is a yogi and leads a vegan lifestyle. On the Today Show, Ellen recently explains why she meditates: "Because it feels good. Kinda like when you have to shut your computer down, just sometimes when it goes crazy, you just shut it down and when you turn it on, it's OK again. That's what meditation is for me."

This is just a brief sampling of the many successful people who have reaped the tremendous benefits of practicing medication and mindfulness every day. Others include William George, Board Member for Goldman Sachs Group Inc., Bob Shapiro formerly the CEO of Monsanto, Tiger Woods, and Russell Brand. These are highly successful people in various fields who have found mediation to be an integral part of their lives, contributing to their success in various ways.

"It changes consciousness," Russell Brand muses about his daily session of meditation plus yoga. "It's really good if you've had addiction issues. It's highly psychological, and very beautiful, and overwhelming, and real, and trippy!" Brand says, "I have become a better person through meditation, and I want to help bring this gift to others. Breathe. Take a look inside yourself."

Chapter 15: The Two Arrows

There is one very important teaching that I would like to talk about in book. It is called the teaching of the two arrows.

The first arrow is pain. Physical or psychological pain, like discomfort or sadness. It is the initial feeling you have.

The second arrow is the thinking about the pain. Fear, worry, all thoughts, such as: "I don't want this", "I don't like this", "It's not fair". So you fire a second arrow into the same route. You fire lots of arrows repeatedly, which becomes more suffering.

When you suffer from a chronic long-term disease or when you have a nervous breakdown, it is really easy to become obsessed with thinking and lost in fear and anxiety, and of course that makes your body and mind less easy to heal.

However, you can learn to watch emotions come and go without reacting negatively.

Do you know how long an emotion lasts?

An emotion lasts up to 90 seconds.

 Think Carefully About This

The longest emotions last 90 seconds, but you feel them for days, months, and years, don't you? Why do you think it happens?

You feel them for a long time because you keep them going. You keep the negative emotions going by thinking about them, by firing the second arrows.

This is really important. If you want to be able to meet trouble and still be creative, you need to learn how to work with emotions and thoughts. You don't want to change them or get rid of them. You just want to be able to work with them. Working with what comes to your door. You don't go looking for trouble, but when it comes to your door you meet it and learn to work with it. You must do it because you'll always have difficult situations in your way. It makes part of life and you can't stop it from happening, but you can learn how to better cope with the situations.

How can you respond to these situations instead of reacting and keep firing the second arrows?

Acceptance

You have done the 3-minute breathing space, but there are other practices to cope with difficult situations.

Don't be surprised or disturbed by what I am going to say. The keyword is "Acceptance". Nowadays much is spoken about acceptance, but what exactly means acceptance?

What do you thing "Acceptance" means?

There is a misconception about the real meaning of this word, which is also a practice. Acceptance is a practice!

Many people think that acceptance is not good, that it means passive resignation, or giving up, or that you have to tolerate injustice just because things "have to be" that way. Not at all! Acceptance does not mean that you have to like everything and abandon your principles and values. It also doesn't mean that you cannot change things or that they are going to be the same forever. It means quite the opposite.

Acceptance simply means that you have come around to a willingness to see things as they are. This attitude sets the stage for responding appropriately in your life, no matter what is happening. You are much more likely to know what to do and have the inner conviction to act when you have a clear picture of what is actually happening, than when your vision is clouded by your mind's judgments, desires, or fears.

Acceptance helps reduce what people experience as negative. In other words, desiring the world to be something it is not is stopped and ruminating thoughts about how things "should be" are put aside. When you have a more clear perspective, then you are more likely to change what can be changed.

Acceptance is an active process. It must be practiced and it takes commitment and motivation to keep this practice. Remember, this motivation is yourself, your wellbeing, your peace, and your mental sanity. Yours and maybe that of your loved ones.

In many cases you have a choice. You can either accept or reject, and much of the time rejecting doesn't change your reality, it just causes pain. Essentially, accepting the "pain" (or the reality, or experience, or relationship) causes less suffering than struggling vainly against it.

This is very hard, but you have to do it for yourself and your loved ones and, because of it being so hard, the question you have to ask yourself is "Can I accept? Can I accept the pain so I limit the suffering?

That's the choice you have. You cannot stop the first arrow. Pain keeps coming and even if you don't accept it, it will still be there. If you are willing to accept and be with whatever is there you reduce the suffering. That could be the suffering of depression, or anxiety, or just the suffering of physical pain, it doesn't matter really. You need to meet the pain so you can stop suffering.

 Think Carefully About This

How do you meet the pain so that you stop the suffering? What is the method to do this?

Chapter 16: Walking Meditation

Walking meditation is a great because it allows you to move. This technique is perfect for people who have a hard time sitting still. Walking meditation is not the same as strolling in the park. Walking meditation requires you to focus on your feet as you move. You also get to hit two birds with one stone as you get to meditate and exercise at the same time. This type of meditation is invigorating, interesting, and it is fun too.

Here's how you can do walking meditation:

Stretch and do a couple of warm up exercise before you begin your meditation practice. You can stretch your legs or your arms. You can do a few yoga poses like the Warrior Pose or the Downward Dog to help stretch your body.

Then, stand still for a minute or two. Take deep breaths. Watch your chest go up and down as you breathe in and breathe out. Take time to notice the sensations in your body, especially in your leg area.

Then, start walking. Pay attention to each of your steps. As soon as your foot touches the ground, take note of any feelings or sensations. Then, as you lift your foot, again take time to notice the sensations.

You'll discover that you feel different types of feelings each time you make a step. There's a different sensation that comes with every step. Remember to notice only the feelings and sensation and refrain from making any judgments.

When distracting thoughts enter your mind during your walking meditation session, simply acknowledge them and then gently shift your focus back to your steps.

You can do this for 10 to 15 minutes. You can walk around the neighborhood or in your local park. You can do this alone and you can do this in groups. As with other forms of mindfulness, you need to do this daily to reap its full results.

Chapter 17: What Do You Need To Meditate With Zazen?

One of the good things about just about any form of meditation is that there is very little equipment needed. You can sit on the floor or use a chair if you have problems getting up and down. Just to get you started, here are a few things you may need.

☐ A comfortable chair or cushion where you can sit with your spine erect. Imagine your head is suspended from the ceiling by a string and let your vertebra hang naturally. Do not sit stiffly.

☐ A quiet place where you will not be disturbed including by other people, or phones, etc.

☐ A timer. You can use the one on your cellphone but be sure to set it to vibrate or hum. Turn off notifications.

☐ A small meditation notebook and pen or pencil.

One question most people ask is "Where do my hands go"? If you are like most of us, we are so used to our hands being busy, it is difficult to find a resting place for them.

The answer is, let them rest anywhere you are comfortable. You can clasp them together, on your thighs, on your knees, or with the palms up. There is no magic position for this.

There are many pictures of hand elegant positions, also known as mudras that practitioners may use. Here are three examples.

Gyan Mudra: used for relaxation and to focus the mind on the task of meditation. The thumb and tip of the pointer finger meet, making an 'ok' sign.

Dhyana Mudra: Thumb tips touch while the backs of one hand's fingers lay lightly on the other hand.

Shuni Mudra: Thumb tip to index fingertip and is used for spiritual and emotional balance and patience.

Meditate with Zazen

Place

Find a quiet place. No distraction and hopefully not a lot of foot traffic where you will not be disturbed.

Positioning

Sitting in a comfortable position or one that you will be able to maintain during the session. You don't want to be so comfortable that you go to dreamland, but comfortable. You can sit cross-legged like a Native American (Half Lotus), Full Lotus (where the tops of your feet rest on top of your thighs), or Burmese (a modified Native American pose where the tops of your feet rest on the ground before you).

Try not to lean to one side or the other and keep your weight equally distributed.

Remember that as you start meditating, your mind will naturally wonder. It's okay if it does because it means your brain is alive and functioning as it usually does.

Thoughts are the reactions to what goes into and out of the brains function. This is what the brain was created for. It also keeps your heart beating and all the other functions to keep us alive. Remember those thoughts will take place on one level or another, and meditation's goal is to shift your focus to being aware of the thought process and what makes up those thoughts.

Meditation is not taking your brain and making it a blank slate. It is about taking the thinking process and expanding it to a new level above the thinking mind. Mental noting is noticing where your mind goes when it wanders around, and consciously bringing it back to focus on the breath.

Set your Intention:

"I will practice breath awareness as a form of meditation for five minutes counting each breath. When my mind wonders, I will return to counting the breath, beginning again with one. (in other words, don't stress if you lose count. Just start over).

Begin Meditating

Set a timer for five minutes.

Gently close your eyes.

Bring awareness to breathe.

Feel your breath as your lungs expand outward and then contract.

Count each inhale until you reach 10, then start over again with one.

Notice the movement of your body during each breath, the expansion and contraction of the lungs, the movement of the rib cage, and all other parts of the body.

Whenever you lose count, simply begin counting again with one. The counting is a focusing agent rather than being important counting how many breathes you take.

When the timer goes off, and you've finished your meditation, take a deep breath, let it out and reach for your notebook. If you have time, you can sit longer, if you wish. You can also use the time to jot down notes about what you experienced during your session.

Putting it all Together

Taking stock of what you experienced during your meditation will help you track how you are doing. If your goal is to meditate every day, this will let you know how your program of meditation is working.

If you are using a paper-based book, there will room at the end of each chapter for you to jot down the basics like the day, the time, the place and how long you spent meditation. If this is not thorough enough for you, keep a small notebook and pen or pencil handy and jot down the results of the following:

☐ How did you feel while meditating?

☐ What kind of thoughts came to mind during the experience?

☐ What do you think you might do differently the next time you try this same technique? Maybe change location, the position of your hands or how long you invested in the session?

☐ Did you experience anything that you did not expect? This could be physical, mental or emotional.

What next?

You can deepen the experience the next time around by following some of these techniques the next time you use this type of meditation:

☐ Take note of your breathing, particularly the exhale, without counting; or, you can count each exhales rather than inhales

☐ Notice changes and feelings in your body while meditating.

☐ Sit even longer than the 20 to 40 minutes twice a day.

☐ Stop thinking about anything other than the task at hand. Breathe. Enjoy what you are doing at that moment rather than thinking of all the tasks ahead.

☐ If someone else is speaking, concentrate on what they are saying. Don't let your mind wander but keep it open and really listen.

☐ Don't think about everything you hate or even like about your job. Just breathe and do your best.

☐ Leave work at work and enjoy your off time with family and friends.

Questions and notes:

The first session of any meditation can be difficult. What problems did you have? Did your mind wonder too much? How did you correct it?

Did you have a problem with the positioning of your hands? Remember that meditation is a practice. What hand position are you thinking of trying next?

What was the most difficult aspect of meditating today? Finding time? The location? Did your mind wonder about other things?

Chapter 18: Anxiety Disorders

Anxiety disorders are the most frequent psychiatric disorders in the world. In the United States, over 28% of adults meet the criteria for an anxiety disorder in their life.

The onset of a stress disorder is normally in childhood, ado-lescence or young adulthood, along with the median age of onset will be 11 decades. Females are typically more likely than males to suffer from anxiety disorders. Stress disorders occur across all racial groups. Anxiety disorders are serious medical illnesses that can be chronic and intense.

Contrary to the relatively mild and short-lived anxiety that occurs with regular stressful events, the anxiety disorders may become overwhelming difficulties and can grow progressively worse if not treated and recognized. According to the National Comorbidity Survey Replication of individuals with anxiety disorders of 12 weeks' duration, overall medical providers treated over 24% of those. The yearly price tag of anxiety disorders is from the billions of dollars and over half the costs are the result of non-psychiatric direct medical expenses including hepatitis or inadequately treated disorders. Enhancing the recognition, diagnosis and treatment of anxiety disorders in primary care is vital to help alleviate the pain, suffering and economic loss associated with all these debilitating disorders that affect one in four U.S. adults.

Anxiety disorders with signs and symptoms:

Panic disorder (with/without agoraphobia)

Agoraphobia without history of panic disorder

Particular phobia

Social phobia (social anxiety disorder)

Obsessive-compulsive disorder

Acute stress disorder

Posttraumatic stress disorder

Generalized anxiety disorder

Stress disorder due to some generalized medical illness

Substance-induced anxiety disorder

Anxiety disorder not otherwise specified

Each anxiety disorder has its own characteristic features, however, the center symptom is the excessive experience of anxiety. Physicians may misunderstand anxiety disorders and not recognize their symptoms, especially since pressure may manifest in different forms. People may feel nervous and worry the majority of the time free of apparent reason, feel tired, have trouble concentrating, uneasy feelings in social conditions, irrational fears or improper ideas, display avoidance behaviors or suffer from periods of intense and frightening feelings that could be immobilizing. Some individuals misinterpret anxious feelings as melancholy. All the anxiety disorders may include some degree of situational stress symptoms. Shared proper (main) anxiety disorders contain generalized anxiety disorder, panic disorder, obsessive-compulsive disorder, phobias (particular, social phobia [social stress disorder]) and posttraumatic stress disorder. Examples of different kinds of anxiety with a concise description along with a summit age period at the onset.

Particular phobias: inborn, conditioned, heard fears, middle childhood.

Social phobias: shyness, social discomfort, middle adolescence.

Panic Disorder: fear attacks late adolescence.

Generalized Stress Disorder: excessive worry young maturity about consequences.

Obsessive-Compulsive Disorder: repetitive early adulthood.

Posttraumatic Anxiety Disorder: stress from childhood/later.

Traumatic Experiences (age of onset depends on occasion).

It's important to differentiate the anxiety disorders from one another and from other psychiatric disorders. The focus of this stress and the specific bunch of symptoms help distinguish among the various stress illness groups. A particular diagnosis may determine particular therapy choices by the clinician. As an instance, it's crucial to start anti-depressants in low dosages and gradually titrate upward into a patient with generalized anxiety disorder and panic disorder to prevent or decrease jitteriness or exacerbation of their stress symptoms. Also higher eventual doses of anti-depressants like selective serotonin reuptake inhibitors may be necessary for the treatment of Obsessive-Compulsive symptoms. Simple phobias are proven usually not to be responsive to medications and need treatment with psychotherapy such as cognitive-behavior treatment.

Stress disorders often coexist with other stress disorders. Packaging the anxiety disorders into nice neat categories is useful; however, the practitioner must remember that actual life demonstrations of these disorders often do not appear within this way. The comorbidity with other disorders such as depression, bipolar disorder, eating disorders, chemical usage disorders and adult attention deficit disorder can complicate both the Identification and therapy of stress disorders. There is also a heightened risk for suicidal behaviors together with comorbid disorders.

It's crucial to consider several factors when assessing a patient for stress disorders. There's an intricate interaction among these facets which includes genetics, emotional and lifestyle experiences in addition to brain chemistry. Although everybody has undergone anxiety and anxiety at the same time or another, not everybody develops a stress disorder. Genetic variations can induce someone to stress disorders. The dopamine transporter gene variation is a good illustration of a particular issue that may result in reduced serotonin levels. There are most likely several genes involved with stress disorders. Family, twin and adoption studies have now demonstrated heredity to become a factor regarding stress disorders. Heredity was known as the late 19th century as an important element in people with anxiety disorders. Those that possess a relative like a sibling or a parent with a stress disorder are at a heightened risk for developing a stress disorder. Researchers are still pursuing genetic linkage info as well as the identification of particular genes and regions of enzymes that could be connected with the exposure to stress disorders.

Psychological factors can also be related to stress disorder symptoms. Individuals prone to stress sensitivity could misinter-free physiological cues. Common bodily symptoms could possibly be misinterpreted because of dangerous or significant problem and this might cause anxiety and stress symptoms. Other psychological facets common to stress disorders incorporate the emotion of stress related conditions linked to the danger of injury and behaviors associated with preventing, preventing or escaping expected harm. For instance, a person may suffer from anxiety attacks and misinterpret the greater heartbeat, chest distress and light-headedness like signs of a heart attack or even a stroke. Concerns about getting another episode may result in anticipatory stress and maybe avoidance of a location or situation connected with an assault in which escape could be termed a difficult or impossible job.

Psychodynamic theories remain as important aspects in the understanding of stress disorders. Janet revealed that stress disorder symptoms caused in the ego diminished by an emotional injury that resulted in a lack of psychological control.

Freud originally theorized that the self as being powerful and resilient from injury and equipped to repress their related painful influence and change them through psychodynamic defenses to psychoneurotic symptoms. Afterwards, Freud analyzed clinical stress and reasoned that stress is bodily and stayed outside the boundaries of psychodynamic theory. A professional who's psychodynamically oriented view points anxiety for a reflection of an inherent psychological battle that may be researched and solved. The main focus contains the individual's ideas, feelings, dreams, feelings and thoughts.

Temperament can also impact a person's disposition to anxiety disorders. Temperament is a composite of emotional reactivity in addition to intellectual, moral and bodily characteristics that stay fairly stable with time. Scientists have noticed that some kids are born with a more moderate prejudice known as behavioral inhibition that doubles as raised physiological reactivity and stress in unfamiliar surroundings.

Environmental and societal factors are included with the development of stress disorders such as learned behaviors. Risk factors for its development of anxiety disorders in children incorporate parental overprotection, excessive complaint and too little warmth. Other ecological risk factors include social isolation, poverty and repeated private losses and vulnerability to violence.

Several neuro-transmitters (chemical messengers) in different regions of the brain are demonstrated to play a part in the neuro-biology of fear and nervousness. Long-term dis-regulation of these chemicals has effects on cortical and subcortical regions and this seems to contribute to the growth of anxiety disorders. Research in animal physiology and human pharmacological studies have indicated that the familiar neurotransmitters γ-aminobutyric acid (GABA), norepinephrine and serotonin are involved in anxiety disorders. Other hormones and neuropeptides that interact and regulate fear and stress comprise CRF, neuropeptide Y, galanin, substance P, many different opioids, dopamine, glutamate, amino acid transmitters and adrenal steroids such as cortisol. Cholecystokinin (CCK), a neuro-peptide found from the gastrointestinal (GI) tract and the mind, is the only circulating endogenous peptide that is proven to be antigenic in people.

All these neuro-chemicals which work in various systems play important adaptive functions in responding to pressure including affecting energy stores, attention, vigilance, memory, planning and cardiovascular functioning. Chronic activation however can be problematic. Clinically many types of drugs are available which influence many of the hormones and therefore are useful in handling the main anxiety disorders. Included in these are the benzodiazepines, serotonin-1A agonists, antidepressants influencing serotonin and norepinephrine.

After a neuron (nerve cell) is triggered, an electric signal travels down the axon and releases a neurotransmitter. The neurotransmitter carries a chemical message across the synaptic cleft attaches to a receptor on the receiving neuron and exerts an excitatory or inhibitory message. Feedback mechanisms serve as regulators for the neurons sending the communications along with a reuptake transporter protein yields the neurotransmitter back across the synapse into the sending neuron after the job is finished. At times this complex system develops problems that manifest clinically as psychiatric illnesses such as anxiety disorders. Issues with neuro-transmission could incorporate receptor hypersensitivity or hyposensitivity, deficient neuro-transmitter release and reuptake occurring too quickly.

As stated before, stress happens as a typical adaptive response to a threat and may be accompanied by improved autonomic (sympathetic and parasympathetic) action. The autonomic nervous system controls involuntary purpose of the inner organs and is involved with the fear response. Abnormal anxiety with physiological activation was demonstrated to add somatic concerns. By way of instance, studies have demonstrated that a history of anxiety disorders is associated with an increased risk for coronary cardiovascular disease such as sudden cardiac death in comparison to a history without anxiety problems.

SEROTONIN SYSTEM

The principal supply of acidity in the central nervous system (CNS) is the raphe nuclei of the brainstem. Serotonin has modulating effects on the locus ceruleus and its projections to the amygdala. It's also associated with cognitive functioning in stress as well as regulating anxiety and impulsivity in suicidal behavior and other violence. Low levels of dopamine can also be connected with dysregulation of other neurotransmitters.

NOREPINEPHRINE (NORADRENERGIC) SYSTEM

The majority of the noradrenergic neurons are found in the locus ceruleus in the dorsal pons. Other regions of the brain that contain noradrenergic neurons incorporate the adrenal gland (hypothalamus, hippocampus and amygdala) in addition to the adrenal gland. Autonomic arousal occurs with stimulation of the locus ceruleus along with the elevated norepinephrine levels are associated with somatic anxiety symptoms like a rapid heartbeat and increased blood pressure. Chronic signs of high noradrenergic function in patients with anxiety disorders include startle reaction, insomnia and anxiety attacks. Anxiety is related to an increase in the norepinephrine metabolite 3-methoxy-4-hydroxy-phenylglycol (MHPG). There is a high concentration of GABA (inhibitory neurotransmitter) receptors around the noradrenergic cell bodies in the locus ceruleus.

Chapter 19: Relaxation And Mindfulness

I remember the first exercise that my instructor asked me to do, and it was very hard, indeed. I was asked to sit quietly for about a quarter of an hour and simply breathe, in through the nostrils and out through the mouth, thinking about nothing except the breathing and the air going in and out of my body. At this stage of learning, you are skeptical, and skeptical thoughts will go through your mind, doubting your ability to do this without thinking thoughts that were related just to the breathing.

The thoughts came, and the thoughts went, but for the first three days of doing this exercise, I was unable to put the thoughts away. I judged the system of breathing that the teacher was explaining. I judged the act of mindfulness and allowed thoughts to come and go, which were both of a negative and positive nature. I didn't see how letting go of those thoughts would achieve anything at all, and I expect you to have the same feelings too. In the book "Eat, Pray, Love" by Elizabeth Gilbert – which was also made into a movie starring Julia Roberts, the heroine of the story recounts her experience in an ashram and described the feelings that she had when she was asked to stop thinking and simply breathe. Because of her past and the breakup of her marriage, she couldn't let go of thoughts about what the marriage amounted to, words that had been said, and the feeling of being tied to the memories. She thought her marriage merited it, but at the end of the day, it was easy to see that her husband had moved on and was living his life without much thought for her. When bad things happen, we often hold onto thoughts and chew them over in quiet moments, taking away the treasure of that moment and leaving it firmly in the past.

For the relaxation exercise, I want you to take off your shoes and lie on the bed. Try to use one pillow instead of two because this puts your airways in the right position to breathe correctly. Lie on your back and place your hands first upon the area of your upper abdomen so that you can feel your body move as you breathe. What you are going to try to achieve is a rhythm of breathing that is regular. Breathe in through the nostrils to the count of 8. Feel the air going into your lungs, and at the same time, you should feel the motion of the upper abdomen as it goes up and down. Keep breathing in this manner until you establish a good rhythm to your breathing. Then place your arms by your sides.

This exercise is called the body scan, and what you are about to do is to try to be conscious of what you are doing all of the time, letting any other thought that does not relate to this event out of your mind. Letting go of thoughts is vital to mindfulness, so the sooner you practice this, the better. It doesn't mean that you will ignore unresolved thoughts. What it means is that now is not the time to address them. Now, close your eyes. This works better in a dimmed room, so if you find yourself distracted, then close the drapes, so you are more relaxed and get back into that position where your arms are by your side, and your breathing rhythm is regular. Now, close your eyes and think of your toes. I want you to flex your toes and then totally relax them so that they feel heavy. The only thoughts that should go through your mind are of the part of the body you are concentrating on and your breath.

Move up to the ankles. Do the same thing. The idea is to go through each part of the body, including knees, hips, waistline, shoulders, fingers, wrists, forearm, upper arm, and right up to your neck. When you have reached the neck, do the same for the ears, eyes, mouth, and nose and then the top of the head and lie very still breathing in the way that you are, while dismissing all thoughts of anything happening outside of that moment.

The reason I have brought this to you as an exercise is that it all helps you to realize the significance of the breath so that when you start to meditate, you will be better prepared and able to let go of excess thoughts so that your meditation benefits you more than it otherwise would. The other power that you gain from being able to drop thoughts is that you can place all of your concentration on a specific job or a task that you have to do and keep concentrating on that task until it is done. Our world today interrupts us far too much, and although you may have alerts waiting for your attention, the time to avoid looking at these is during a specific task or when you are trying to relax. You can give them your attention as a task later on, and learning to cut off the interruptions the world imposes on you is great while you are learning to use mindfulness in your life.

You become more focused in your life and are able to do things that you only dreamt about in the past because you free up so much time – time wasted on thoughts that serve no purpose in your life. When you stop fighting that part of your thinking process, everything changes with it, and you become more comfortable with who you are and what you feel about life and your relationship with it. When it was suggested that it was all about getting to know yourself, I thought of the sixties, when people first went out to "find" themselves, and they were looking in the right direction, though many of the practices of those times did not achieve the same as mindfulness meditation does.

If you find that you are stressed from time to time, doing the body scan as described in this chapter will help you to get beyond that feeling. It will help you to be able to relax, and you must remember if you don't do this at bedtime, remember to give your body time to get back to its normal breathing pattern before you get up as your heart rate becomes slower and your blood pressure will be lower.

Chapter 20: Deeper Practice

The two elements of mindful meditation you've learned thus far, breathing and the body scan, will be combined to form an entire practice in this chapter. Don't rush into this practice because it takes time to build up to. You should ideally spend a month practicing the previous exercises separately and living in a mindful manner before adopting the full practice of sitting meditation.

This practice takes you deeper into the mindfulness realm and is accompanied by some yoga poses as well to help you ease your way into it. Your body will most likely not be able to adjust to the requirements of the meditation which is why practicing yoga is a good idea.

In addition to yoga, there are some theoretical points you need to understand as well. These deal with the various aspects of sitting meditation. So, let's begin by looking at these in detail.

Elements

Sitting meditation is pretty much what you think it is. You sit there and contemplate with awareness. The practice itself is far more active than that though. You see, contemplation is not an easy task and you need to work hard at it. We're used to grasping at things and doing things to gain achievements that it takes time to adjust to doing nothing to achieve something.

You will be contemplating every facet of your experience, from breathing to smells to sensations. Each of these have their own vagaries, so understanding them will improve your overall experience.

Breathing

Every mindfulness practice starts with the breath. Truth be told, your breath is more than enough to tell you everything you need to know about your existence. You see, your breath is constantly in motion and is ever-changing. It illustrates a basic truth about this world. The more you try to hold onto something, the more you increase your suffering.

Anyone who tries to hold their breath is simply signing up for some suffering. Eventually, you're going to give in and gulp air in large quantities. Mindful awareness of your breath is all about being with it and observing it. It is allowing it to ebb and flow and not bother about controlling it in any way. This is how we need to approach change in our lives as well.

The only constant in this world is change and your ability to deal with change is directly linked to how much stress you hold within yourself. The worse your ability, the greater the stress you'll experience. Observing your breath teaches you that pushing things you don't like away from you and pulling things you do wish to have in your life only creates a vicious circle of wanting and regret.

This push/pull dynamic is what causes suffering. The key to your whole world lies in understanding your breath. Mindfulness meditation aims to open your eyes to this fact.

Sensations

In the body scan, you went through each part of your body to discover the presence of any sensations. Sitting meditation moves from awareness of your breath to awareness of sensations. This does not refer to just the sensations you feel in individual parts of your body but as a whole.

Much like your breath, the sensations you feel are constant. There is always something the environment is transmitting to you via your sense organs and these ebb and flow like your breath. Not a single one of them is permanent. This adds another layer of understanding to the one you gained by observing your breath.

While your breathing mechanism is permanent, the sensations you experience are not. Moreover, there are many layers to the sensations you feel, from gross obvious ones to more subtle ones which lie beyond your consciousness. At higher levels of awareness, you'll become very aware of how your body is just a collection of vibrations and that what you think of as solid and real really isn't. However, this is something that has to be experienced through practice and cannot be simply described.

Hearing

Sounds are external sensations in the sense that they are not created within our body. Sure, some sounds are but the large majority of things we perceive through our ears originate from outside of us. This is yet another lesson in impermanence and of how change is constant.

At its heart, mindfulness aims to get you to understand how everything changes and that placing a lot of stock on things which shift all the time is an unwise way to live. As we go about our day, we encounter all sorts of noises that irritate us. Dogs barking, horns honking, construction noises and so on.

Mindfulness teaches you to recognize the impermanence of these things and to let them bounce off you or pass through you.

Noise and sound are something you cannot escape. If you tried to shut your ears and wore earmuffs or earplugs, you'd still hear your pulse and other noise produced by bodily functions. Instead of trying to push them away, accept them and recognize that they will soon die away. Practice this during your meditation.

Thoughts

After contemplating noises, your thoughts are where your attention will turn to. Thoughts rule us as we've seen thus far in this book. Dealing with them is no small feat and yet it's amazing how so many of our thoughts are impermanent and simply don't matter very much in the grand scheme of things.

There are many kinds of thoughts you will become aware of as well as the emotions that go along with them. Emotions bring their own weight to the table and it is very hard to ignore them. You see, this is why ignorance and indifference don't work. You can ignore noises and sounds, you can choose to be unaware of your breath and sensations, but there is no escaping your thoughts.

The mistake lies in assuming that your thoughts are you. When practicing mindfulness, you're observing yourself and are hence forcing a third person point of view on your activities. This is what makes it easy for you to uncouple your sense of identity from your thoughts.

The sense of "I" vanishes when you view your thoughts mindfully. They're impermanent, like everything else, and hardly ever represent who you are. An interesting question to ask is what the nature of "you" is, but this isn't a philosophical book. In terms of understanding where your stress originates from, the conflict between your thoughts and the feedback from the outside world is the biggest source of stress.

Becoming aware of the impermanence of your thoughts is a huge step for you to take and this is something that only comes from repeated practice. In addition to recognizing thoughts which cause conflict, you'll also observe thoughts which pigeonhole you into neat looking brackets which cause conflict.

Things such as cars, homes, money and so on are mere brackets of limiting beliefs your mind is imposing on you. Why it does this is not your concern. It does it and you experience conflict which prompts stress. Recognize how you have a choice and that there's never just one correct answer to everything. A different perspective can provide insight that greatly reduces stress and offers a deep view into the nature of things.

This is what mindfulness is really all about.

Awareness

This is the final element of mindful meditation and is the summation of everything else we've talked about so far.

In this state, you're supremely aware of the validity of the present moment and can see that your life is a collection of "nows." You're not judging anything, and life unfolds itself as a river that flows past you.

You're sitting on the bank watching it go by and are noting everything that is floating on it. It could be tree bark, or it could be an alligator, it doesn't matter. It's floating past and you're observing it since you're not emotionally invested in it.

You do feel emotions, for example, if the alligator decides to shift course and turn you into its lunch. However, you're not building this attack into something it isn't. You're not turning around and thinking that the river is full of alligators. How can it be? In the present moment, just one is attacking you. You have no other concerns for now.

In the state of awareness, you'll be supremely aware of how your mind and body are working together and how your existence is interacting with them. You'll notice how various things come together to form what you think of as reality and how little control you have over many of them.

You'll recognize that impermanence is the state of things and that this is perfectly fine.

Sitting Meditation

As you read this meditation, pay special attention to the paragraphs. These are pauses where you should practice what has just been said before moving forward. A good idea is to record these on tape in your own voice and then play it back with appropriate pauses between the paragraphs.

Pat yourself on the back for dedicating this time to your mindfulness practice.

Gradually, move into the present moment. As you do, notice and regard with equanimity any thoughts you are carrying with regards to what has happened in your day thus far or what happened previously. Notice them and explore their nature.

Now, gradually let them be. Let them be present and recognize that they have a right to be present. You hold no ill will or negative feeling towards them. Just let them remain where they are, as they are.

Once this is done, shift your awareness to your breath. Notice your inhalation and exhalation. Notice the nature of it and take note of whether you're breathing fully into your stomach or your diaphragm. Don't modify your breath in any way or try to control it. Just notice it and become aware of it.

Move your awareness to the portion of your face that is between the nose and the upper lip. Notice how the air you breathe out strikes it. Don't control your breath in any way but keep observing this area and keep scanning it for any sensations along with your breath striking it. Move one inhalation and one exhalation at a time. This is all you're aware of.

Move gently onto your entire body and scan it as a whole for any sensations you feel. Simply take note of them and observe their nature. Don't explore each and every part of your body but your entire physical presence. Do not judge or label anything. Just observe.

Notice any areas of tension or tightness and see if you can relax them. If you can't, that's fine, simply notice them and allow them to be. Some sensations might exhibit a wave-like nature. Let them go where they want to go and restrict nothing.

Next, move your awareness to the sounds you can hear, whether they be external or internal. Notice how they're merely waves which bounce off you. Observe them with equanimity and recognize how none of them are good or bad in and of themselves. It is your labels that make them good or bad.

Remain in this state of acknowledgement and continue to focus on these sounds. Notice how they rise and fall. Notice how they're impermanent. They might seem steady to you, but on closer inspection, you recognize the ups and downs of the sound waves that are a part of them.

Now, move your awareness to your mind and take note of the emotions you're feeling. Allow them to pass by, like boats on a river, and notice how they change and morph constantly as they struggle to capture your attention. Notice how your mind distorts and twists things just to entrap you.

These emotions rise and fall and then rise again. They are impermanent. Yesterday they were saying one thing and today it's something else. Tomorrow, there will be something else to moan about. This is perfectly fine. Smile at them and wave them as the move past you.

If you fall into one of these thoughts or emotions, once you're aware of them, bring your awareness back to your observation post and simply watch as thoughts go by. Notice that the mind is almost a separate entity from you entirely. It has its own nature and can act like a wounded animal at times. Notice how it generates its own stories and traps for you to walk into.

If you repeatedly fall for the mind's traps, don't admonish yourself. If anything, you are to be congratulated because you keep realizing awareness every time you return to your observation post. This is a very good thing, so be proud of yourself. Keep observing the impermanence of the state of things.

Now, bring your awareness to the entire body and mind of your being. You are now focusing on the present moment entirely. This is the sum of sensations, emotions, thoughts and sounds you are currently perceiving. Look at them as a whole. Notice how everything is constantly changing chaotically. Can you see why you've been carrying so much stress? You've been trying to make sense of this chaos. Simply continue to observe the chaos around you as it keeps changing, ever in flux.

Don't worry about focusing on a particular thing. If no sensation or thought makes itself available to you in the moment, switch your attention to your breathing. Don't force or change anything, just observe it and acknowledge it.

After spending some time in this state of acknowledging the present moment and noticing its impermanence, bring your awareness back to your breath. Notice your inhalation and exhalation. Withdraw your awareness from it and gently open your eyes.

Congratulate yourself on having completed this meditation. Journal your experiences and reflect on what you have observed and learned.

Yoga for Meditation

Yoga and meditation are deeply connected to one another. Ancient texts originating from modern day India record how monks were able to meditate better and longer thanks to practicing yoga. A lot of yoga is derived from observing how animals behave in nature and the poses work to release pent up energy in the body.

Practicing yoga by itself is a form of meditation. The poses I'll be listing here are helpful in making you more flexible so that your sitting meditation doesn't have to be as painful as it was the first time you did it.

Supine Stretches

Lie on your back on the floor with your arms out to your sides and palms facing upwards. Take a few deep breaths and exhale. Now, sweep your arms out to above your head with your palms facing one another. Take a deep breath as you do so. Exhale as you bring your arms back down by your side. Repeat this for four or five breaths.

Once this is done extend your arms out to the side with the palms facing upwards. With your feet on the ground, bring your knees upwards and fold them towards you. Now take a deep breath and lower your knees to your right while keeping the upper half of your body straight.

As you do this, turn your head to the left and exhale. Bring your knees back to the middle and then lower them to the left while turning your head to the right. Do this for four or five breaths. When doing this, notice any emotions or sensations you feel and allow them to pass through.

Once done, lower your knees to the ground and bring your arms above your head with palms facing one another. Inhale and exhale deeply for a few breaths.

Leg Stretch

Lying on the floor, bend your left knee while keeping your foot on the ground. Lift your right leg straight up with your heel pointing to the ceiling. Now as you breathe normally, flex your ankle and try to get your toes pointing towards the ceiling. Now rotate your ankle in either direction and bring your leg down.

Repeat the process with your other leg. Perform the same pose four more times for each leg.

Pelvic Tilt

While lying on the ground, bring both of your knees up while keeping your feet on the floor. Press gently on your tailbone and inhale. You should feel a small gap between your lower back and the floor. As you exhale, let your lower back fall to the floor again. Repeat this four or five times. From this, transition into the bridge pose.

Lift your buttocks, your lower back and then your upper back off the floor while keeping your feet planted on the floor and inhale. Bring your arms underneath your body and interlock your fingers. Spend three breaths in this position and then slowly lower your body back down, thinking of it as lowering one vertebra at a time in a gradual motion.

Repeat this five times. Notice any emotions or energy shifts as you do this.

Bird Dog Pose

Get up off the floor and kneel down. Move your torso forward and support yourself by placing your arms perpendicular to the floor. Make sure your arms are positioned below your shoulders.

Now, extend your left leg backwards until it is straight and simultaneously lift your right arm upwards while keeping it straight. Think of your right arm, torso and leg forming a straight line when looked at from the side. Hold the position for five breaths and repeat with your other leg and arm.

Repeat this process five times each side.

Corpse Pose

Always end your yoga session with this pose. Stillness is as important in yoga as movement is. Lie down on your back with your arms out to the side with palms facing upwards. Take stock of everything in your body and travel through it, taking note of sensations along with any thoughts or feelings you are experiencing.

Breathe naturally and deeply into your stomach. Feel the energy coursing through you and lie in this position for a couple minutes. Give thanks and open your eyes.

You can expand your yoga practice to include more poses than these. At a minimum, practice these poses since they release energy in your body and allow its free flow. If your hips and ankles hurt after sitting on the floor, or if you find that your knees do not lie flat on the ground in the lotus position, work on unlocking your hips and improving their flexibility.

Conclusion

We've addressed a whule lot within this book but, ideally, you now recognize that mindfulness is a lot more than just a potent form of meditation. Sure, it is that also, but beyond this mindfulness simply indicates being more familiar with your own thoughts, your own body and your own views and visualizations. Whenever we accomplish this, it enables us to choose how we wish to feel, how we intend to act and what we would like to think. Rather than allowing the body and mind be reactive to our environment, we rather learn to second-guess ourselves and to ensure we are in the ideal attainable mindset and mood for the current situation.

That could mean being more vigilant so we can concentrate on work. It might imply being calmer for our wellness and for our social connections. It might indicate being more inspired for the gym. Or it could just mean being a little kinder to ourselves or altering the way we speak.

Mindfulness is the trick to uncovering the complete potential of your mind and body. And whenever you can accomplish that, all sorts of doors begin to open for you.

www.ingramcontent.com/pod-product-compliance
Lightning Source LLC
Chambersburg PA
CBHW072008070526
44583CB00015B/1383